King of the Cannibals

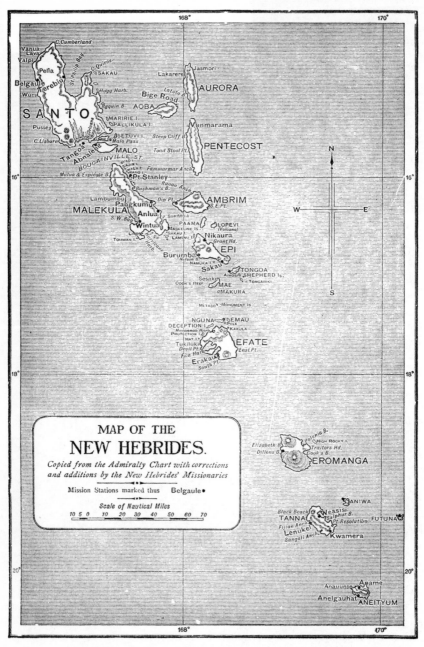

A map of the New Hebrides from John Paton's time

King of the Cannibals

The story of John G. Paton
Missionary to the New Hebrides (Vanuatu)

Jim Cromarty

 EVANGELICAL PRESS

Solid Ground Christian Books

EVANGELICAL PRESS
Faverdale North Industrial Estate, Darlington, DL3 0PH, England

Evangelical Press USA
P. O. Box 84, Auburn, MA 01501, USA

e-mail: sales@evangelicalpress.org

web: http://www.evangelicalpress.org

SOLID GROUND CHRISTIAN BOOKS
PO Box 660132, Vestavia Hills, AL 35266
(205) 978-9469
Solid-ground-books@juno.com
http://solid-ground-books.com

First published 1997
Second impression 2002

British Library Cataloguing in Publication Data available

ISBN 0 85234 401 5

Printed and bound in Great Britain by Creative Print and Design
Wales, Ebbw Vale.

To our dear friends of the Hunter/Barrington Congregation
who supported us for many years with their prayers and
encouraging words

Contents

List of illustrations

Preface

John G. Paton lived in an age of exploration. It was the time of Queen Victoria and people used proudly to boast that the sun never set on the British empire, because it stretched right round the world. In those days British sea-power was so great that it was unchallenged anywhere in the world and the arrival of a British battleship at one of the South Sea Islands was enough to strike terror into the hearts of the inhabitants. But Britain's true greatness lay, not in her navy, but in the efforts of her missionaries to take the gospel of the Lord Jesus Christ to all the world.

John Paton was one of those brave men and women who willingly risked everything, even their lives, in order that the peoples of the world might come to know Christ as Lord and Saviour. His story demonstrates how God protected and cared for one of his faithful servants as he took the gospel to the people of Tanna and Aniwa, islands of the New Hebrides (now called Vaniatu). It is a story that should thrill the hearts of all who read it, because the God who watched over John Paton is the same God who cares for his people today. Our God is all-powerful! This is a truth that John Paton was to prove time and time again.

John led a very exciting life. He lived through times of real heartbreak, but he also knew what it was to experience great joy, and despite the many occasions when his life was in danger he lived to tell the tale and write his own autobiography.

This book is intended as an introduction to John Paton's life. I hope it will encourage readers of all ages to want to go on to read for themselves the full story, as told in his own words, of how God watched over him and cared for him as he worked among primitive cannibal tribesmen and taught them about the one true God and salvation through faith in the Lord Jesus Christ.

I pray that God will be pleased to bless this story to the soul of everyone who reads it, so that you too may come to love and trust the God whom John Paton served so faithfully.

Jim Cromarty

Acknowledgements

Most of the material for this book is taken from *John G. Paton, Missionary to the New Hebrides — An Autobiography,* edited by his brother James Paton, and published by the Banner of Truth Trust, Edinburgh, reprinted 1994.

Some details, relating mainly to his family and to daily life on Aniwa, are taken from *Letters and Sketches from the New Hebrides,* by Margaret Whitecross Paton (ed. James Paton, published by Hodder & Stoughton, London, 1896). Most of the illustrations of scenes and people on the islands were originally used in this book or in *The Story of John G. Paton Told for Young Folks* (Hodder & Stoughton, 1906) also edited by his brother James Paton.

Unless otherwise indicated, quotations are taken from the *Autobiography* or the *Letters and Sketches,* but the English has been very slightly modernized in a few instances of quoted speech, where the original language spoken was not English, so that the words quoted were in any case only a translation.

Special thanks must go to Anne Williamson who helped greatly with the preparation of the manuscript. And thanks to Val who proof-read the work and encouraged me to go on when I became weary.

Thanks are also due to the staff of Dumfries Museum and the Information and Archives department of Dumfries and Galloway Libraries, for their courtesy in allowing photographs of objects and illustrations held by them to be reproduced in this book.

Restored thatched cottage, Torthorwald.

This would have been typical of the cottages in the village in John's boyhood and probably also similar to the one in which he was born.

1.
A Scottish country childhood

John Gibson Paton, whom Charles Spurgeon once referred to as 'the King of the Cannibals', was born on a farm at Braehead,¹ near Dumfries in south-west Scotland, on 24 May 1824. Young John was not born in a hospital, but in a cottage where his parents lived and his father worked as a stocking manufacturer, weaving warm, woollen stockings for the merchants of Hawick and Dumfries to sell to their customers.

John was given his middle name after a wealthy farmer who lived in the big house nearby and was a friend of the family. When he was old enough to walk, John would often wander across the open fields to the Gibsons' mansion. The farmer's wife grew very fond of the little boy she often found playing in her garden and used to make a big fuss of him.

When John was five years old the family moved to the village of Torthorwald. If he climbed a hill near their new home, John could see the village spread out below him, with each cottage standing in its own well-kept garden plot and the smoke from the peat-fires curling up from the cottage chimneys. If he looked carefully he might even see the tiny figures of the villagers coming and going, or standing around in groups on the village green chatting and trying to solve the world's problems.

Torthorwald was a busy, thriving village where everyone had to work hard to earn a living. There were a number of farms, of various sizes, employing both permanent and seasonal labourers. Other villagers worked in their cottages, sitting all day at looms weaving cloth or stockings, or they made shoes for the better-off people and clogs for the peasants to wear. Then there were coopers, who made wooden barrels and casks, and of course, the village blacksmith. Other people were employed at the mill, which was always busy because all the local farmers used to bring their corn there to have it ground to produce flour.

From the hill above the village John could also see the shining church spires and roofs of the buildings in the town of Dumfries, just over four miles away. In the distance he could make out the white sands of the Solway, and on a really clear day he could even see the hills of northern England away over on the far side of the Firth. If he looked inland he could see scattered farms and villages, with a river meandering through open countryside, while on the horizon loomed the dark outline of the Galloway hills. He could also spy the remains of several castles, including the ruins of Lochmaben castle, which used to be the family home of the Scottish hero Robert the Bruce, and what was left of the splendid medieval fortress of Caerlaverock Castle. Seeing these ruins reminded him of the exciting tales that used to be told around the peat fires on long winter evenings about the many battles that were fought and the daring raids that had been carried out in that part of Scotland in years gone by.

The Paton family home was a thatched cottage in the main street of Torthorwald. It was a simple, three-roomed building, constructed around a framework of eight huge oak beams securely fixed in the ground and sloping towards each other at the top to form a pointed roof. Between these beams stone walls, held together by a mixture of sand, clay and lime, had

View of Dumfries and the River Nith, about 1832
Reproduced by courtesy of Dumfries Museum

PATON'S COTTAGE, TORTHORWALD.

The Paton family cottage, Torthorwald. (The cottage has since been demolished)
Reproduced by courtesy of Dumfries and Galloway Libraries, Information and Archives

been built. Young shoots from oak trees were woven together into a kind of matting to form a basis for the roof, which was covered with a solid thatch that kept the inside of the house warm and dry in all weathers. The thatch was kept in good repair and replaced nearly every year.

In front of the cottage there was a small garden and on the opposite side of the road another, much larger, one. Between them, these gardens kept the family well supplied with fresh vegetables. John's mum loved flowers, so no doubt there was always a good show of colourful flowers, too.

The room at one end of the Patons' house was Dad's workshop and in it five or six pairs of hands and feet were kept busy all day long at the frames used for making stockings.

At the other end was Mum's room. This served as the dining room, kitchen and living room all rolled into one. It also contained a couple of large wooden beds, hung around with curtains and covered with brightly coloured bedcovers which John's mother had made, where the children used to sleep. It was here that the family spent many happy hours.

In between the two there was a smaller room where Mum and Dad slept. In it were a small table, a chair and a bed. This room was of special importance to the family because it was the sanctuary of the home, where Dad would often go, especially after meals, to read the Scriptures and seek the face of God in prayer. When Dad had 'shut the door' everyone knew that it was time to be quiet. The children soon learned to go around on tiptoe during Dad's prayer-time so as not to disturb him.

John's mum and dad were the proud parents of eleven children — five sons and six daughters — of whom John was the eldest. The family home at Torthorwald was a true place of security and happiness. John's parents were Christians and it was there in the home that John first became aware of, and came to trust in, the God of heaven and earth who sent his Son into the world to save sinners.

The life of the family was centred around the worship and service of the Lord Jesus Christ. Each day, morning and evening, they would all gather together for family worship. Dad would take down from the shelf the big family Bible and, after the family had joined in singing one or more of the metrical psalms, he would read aloud a passage of Scripture. Following this there would be an explanation and discussion of the Bible passage that had been read. Family worship would then be concluded with prayer. No matter how busy the family members were, even when there were people coming and going, they always made sure that they found time to pray together.

John's dad, James Paton, had wanted to be a minister of the gospel, but circumstances had prevented that coming to pass. However, he longed not only to see all his children following Christ, but also that at least some of his sons should be called to the Christian ministry. Although John did not know this until he was much older, on the day that he was born his parents solemnly gave him back to the Lord in prayer, to serve him overseas as a missionary, if that should be God's will. Those prayers were to be answered in a wonderful way, for not only was John himself one day to be a missionary, but two of his younger brothers also grew up to serve the Lord in the Christian ministry.

John and his brothers and sisters often heard their father praying for their salvation, as well as for the heathen people in distant lands who had never heard the gospel. Even when he was still only a young boy John began to cherish the hope that one day he might, by God's grace, have the privilege of taking the gospel to some part of the world where the inhabitants lived without the knowledge of Christ.

Another view of the Paton family cottage, Torthorwald.
Reproduced by courtesy of Dumfries and Galloway Libraries, Information and Archives

Inside of restored thatched cottage, Torthorwald, showing oak beams which form the basic structure of the house

The home in which John Paton and his brothers and sisters grew up was a happy one of love and affection. Of course, there were times when one or more of the children had to be punished. When that happened John's father would first go to his 'sanctuary' and there pray for God's wisdom that he might do what was right. Then before dealing out the punishment he would carefully explain the reason for what he was about to do.

When the family were all together in the evenings much of their discussion centred around the Scriptures and the saving work of Jesus Christ, but they also found time to laugh and talk together about everyday happenings and to remember amusing incidents which had happened to various members of the family.

John's father, who was called James, enjoyed retelling the story of how he had first met his wife, Janet. As a young man, he used to like to find a quiet spot in the wood where he could spend time reading and praying. As well as studying God's Word he would also read aloud from a book of poems by Ralph Erskine called *Gospel Sonnets*. Those verses so thrilled his mind and soul that he learned them by heart. Then he would take off his hat and kneel down to pray. As he did so, he was totally oblivious of all that was going on around him.

Little did he know that his activities were being watched by a young girl called Janet Jardine Rogerson. She lived with her great-aunt and uncle, who were nicknamed 'Old Adam and Eve' by those who knew them. She used to watch James, the good-looking young stocking-maker, as he came to his special place among the trees to read and pray.

One day, while he was praying, Janet quietly crept up to the spot where he had left his hat, removed it and hung it on a branch of a nearby tree. When he had finished his devotions, it took James some time to find his hat. He was very puzzled as to where it could be. Maybe he thought he was growing forgetful! The next day Janet did the same thing and once again James spent a long time looking about among the trees and undergrowth before he found his hat.

After she had hidden James' hat for a second time, Janet began to feel sorry for this young man to whom she had never spoken, and who was so obviously disturbed as a result of the joke she had played on him. So the next day she fixed a note to the tree where James always knelt in prayer. In it she wrote, 'She who stole your bonnet is ashamed of what she did; she has a great respect for you, and asks that you pray for her, that she may become as good a Christian as you.'

James loved to tell this story. He used to say that until he found her note he had thought an angel must have stolen his hat. However, when he looked around, with the note in his hand, he soon saw the lovely 'angel' in front of 'Adam's cottage', swinging a milk-pail and singing as she walked along. It wasn't long before he made her acquaintance. When James told this tale, Janet would blush and laugh and playfully tell him to be quiet. Sometimes she would tease him in return, asking why, if he really wanted to be alone, he had chosen that particular spot in the woods in which to read and pray. John's mum and dad truly loved each other and their love filled the home with great joy.

Another time one of John's parents would tell the story of James' father, who as a young man had been seized by the press-gang and forced to serve as a sailor on a British man-of-war. He had been captured in one of their battles with the French and had ended up as a sailor on a ship where the captain was a notorious pirate, called Paul Jones. For the rest of his life he carried a great scar on his shoulder, where the captain had once slashed him with his sword in a fit of temper. The story of their grandfather's escape from the pirates and his many other adventures before his eventual return to Scotland was

Caerlaverock Castle.

Tales of this and other historic sites in the area were told around the fireside in the evenings.

one that thrilled the hearts of the children as they all sat around the fire in the evening.

Janet also had a tale to tell about her mother and father. Her father, William Rogerson, was a blacksmith. He fell in love with a girl called Janet Jardine, who was from a wealthy family. Janet's uncles, who were responsible for her as her parents were dead, thought a mere blacksmith not good enough for their niece and would not give the couple permission to marry. However, William rode up on horseback with a party of his friends and stole her away. The couple then married and were very happy together, but Janet lost her inheritance as her uncles sold everything she owned and then emigrated to the New World with the proceeds. When William heard about the sale, he dashed off on horseback to confront them, but the only thing he was able to rescue was the family Bible, which was just being put up for auction at the very moment he arrived.

These stories must have thrilled young John, but little did he know that the day would come when he too would have thrilling stories to recount to those who sat at his knee listening to him recalling his adventures and God's goodness to him.

1. From John's reference in his *Autobiography* to the parish of Kirkmahoe, his birthplace was evidently the Braehead near Dalswinton, a few miles to the north-west of Dumfries, rather than the place of the same name just south of Torthorwald (*Publishers' note*).

To think about

John's early life shows us that every detail of our lives is planned by God. He has a purpose for each person who exists. For those who become Christ's disciples there is a pathway of service ahead for which he prepares us very carefully. Every detail of our upbringing and education, where we live, our families and what kind of home we are brought up in is used to make us better servants of Jesus Christ. Sometimes those things that we think are unpleasant are ways of preparing us for special tasks ahead. I am sure that John Paton's simple, practical, even hard, family life, without luxury or extravagance, made him into a tougher and more resourceful missionary later on.

Perhaps the greatest blessing that John enjoyed was the privilege of a Christian home and parents who prayed for him and taught him the Scriptures. What kind of upbringing have you had? How might God be preparing you for service to his glory? Have you become a disciple of Jesus Christ? Maybe your family life is not a Christian one, but God has given you Christian friends from whom you can learn much. Pray that God will lead you in every choice and that you may serve him in everything that you do.

2.
Going to church and school

When John stood on the hill and looked down over Torthorwald one of the buildings that caught his eye was the manse, which was half hidden from view among a clump of very old trees. The name 'manse' was a short form of 'the man's house' — that is, the house in which 'the man of God' lived, and it was the name usually used in Scotland to describe the minister's home.

Close by was the village school and a little further away the church building. Beside the church was the graveyard, where crumbling headstones, dating back over some 500 years, told of people long dead who had once been part of the local community.

The Paton family, however, did not attend the parish church. They were members of the Reformed Presbyterian Church and their place of worship was in the town of Dumfries. In those days there was no public transport, and as the Paton family were not rich enough to own their own carriage, Dad and the older children would walk the four miles each way to and from church each Sabbath, as Sunday, or the Lord's Day, was always called in Scotland.

John's father was very regular in his attendance at the services. In the forty years that he lived at Torthorwald he missed worship in Dumfries on only three occasions. Once the

Torthorwald parish church

Old graves in Torthorwald churchyard
John's parents and other members of his family are buried here.

snow was so deep that he just could not find his way and had to turn back. Another time the pathway was covered with ice, making it so slippery that he fell down several times and was eventually forced to abandon the journey and return home because of the danger of injury. On the way back he had to get down on his hands and knees and crawl for part of the way where the track climbed up a steep hillside.

The third occasion involved an outbreak of cholera in Dumfries. A group of people from the village came to the door and begged John's mother to persuade her husband to stay at home for once, because they were afraid that if he were to attend worship in the town he would risk catching that deadly disease and passing it on to others in the village. The neighbours need not have worried, as John's father did not want to put other people in danger, so he willingly remained at home in order to avoid the risk of spreading the disease.

John truly loved the Lord's Day. It was never a dull, wearisome day for him or his family, as it was in some households where people even pulled the blinds down to keep the sun out of the house. For the Patons, Sunday was a truly joyful day specially devoted to the worship of God.

John used to enjoy the walk to Dumfries with his father and brothers and sisters. They would be joined by other Christians who attended various evangelical churches in the town and the children liked listening to the conversations of the adults as they walked along. They were all keen to talk about the sermons they had heard and John could see that their Christian faith was very real to them, influencing the way they lived. He and the other children also enjoyed getting a glimpse of life in a town, which was very different from that back home in their village.

Because of the long walk, John's mother was unable to attend worship except when some friendly neighbour offered her a lift to town in their gig (a two-wheeled carriage light

The road from Torthorwald to Dumfries today. The Paton family would
probably have followed a similar route, since the village lay on an
established coach route from Lockerbie to Dumfries.

The church building where the Paton family worshipped still stands but
is no longer used as a place of worship

enough to be drawn by a single horse). So she would usually stay at home with the younger children. However, her husband and the children who had attended worship made sure that Mum knew everything that had taken place. On the Sunday evening when they all gathered for a special time of family worship, Dad would stride backwards and forwards across the stone-flagged floor of the living room as he repeated the main points of the sermon for his wife's benefit, with the children eagerly joining in to help him along, whenever he stopped or asked them a question. John and his brothers and sisters were encouraged to take notes during the preaching of the sermon and this helped them remember what they heard, especially as they would sit down and get out their notes to read when they returned home.

On Sunday evenings, as well as a Bible reading and a discussion on the Catechism, in which the whole family took part, there would often be talk about a Bible story or a reading of some Christian book, such as *Pilgrim's Progress*. The children would all vie with each other to have a turn at reading aloud while the others listened.

One incident from John's schooldays that he was to remember for the rest of his life concerned an event which occurred when his father was 'taking the books', that is, leading family worship.

Torthorwald had a village school which had a good reputation for learning. It was attended by the children of both rich and poor alike. Education was valued by all and learning and character-building were respected and encouraged. The schoolteacher at the time when John was a boy was a Mr Smith. He had built an extra room onto the school-building and took in students from the surrounding area as boarders.

Although in some ways a good teacher, Mr Smith was also very strict, and at times was very cruel to his students. But there was also a kinder side to his nature, as John discovered.

Torthorwald school, smithy and castle

Mr Smith knew that the Paton family were not so well off as some of the other families whose children attended the school and he could evidently see that John needed new clothes. One night during family worship Mr Smith arrived at the door of the cottage with a new suit of clothes for John. As the family were kneeling at prayer, Mr Smith very quietly lifted the latch of the door and put the parcel of clothes just inside, where John would be sure to find them. No one saw him, but as soon as they got up from their knees John rushed to the door where he found the parcel. We can imagine the surprise and delight of the family when they opened it and found the new set of warm clothes.

The next day, when John arrived at school wearing his new suit, Mr Smith complimented him on his appearance. John told him that God had sent the clothes to him while his dad was reading the Scriptures and praying. Mr Smith laughed and replied, 'John, whenever you need anything after this just tell your father to "tak' the Book" and God will send an answer to your prayers.' It was not till many years later that John found out that it was Mr Smith himself who had brought the parcel.

John was learning through this and other experiences that the God whom he and his parents loved was the God who did the 'impossible' and was capable of providing for all his needs. He was soon to have this wonderful truth further impressed upon his young heart in another remarkable way.

One day, when his father had gone to Hawick to sell some of the goods made in his workshop, food ran out in the Paton household. It was a time when the potato crop in the area had failed and it had been a bad year for other crops too. Many families did not have enough to eat that year, because they depended on the vegetables and other crops they grew in their gardens and on their farms, as the food in the shops cost more than they could afford. In the Paton home the barrel where the flour was kept was empty and there was nothing left in the house for them to eat. That night the children went to bed hungry.

I'm sure that John's mother must have had tears in her eyes when she told the children there was nothing for them to eat. However, it was with a quiet confidence in God that she promised them that in the morning there would be plenty of food on the table. She could say that because she had gathered the family together to pray and had told God of their desperate need. She pleaded with their heavenly Father to provide their daily food. Then she told the children that the next day God would supply them with the food they needed.

I can imagine that when the children had gone to bed that night John's mother knelt once again in prayer, pleading with God to send food to the family. Then she too went to bed, trusting in the goodness of God to answer her prayers. And God did indeed answer her prayers.

Early the next morning, a carrier arrived from Lockerbie, where her father lived, bringing several large packages for the family. Some days earlier, before the barrel of flour had even run out, God had stirred the heart of John's grandfather (who knew nothing about the particular problems the family were having at that moment), to send a parcel of food to his daughter as a present. God had answered her prayer before it was even offered.

There must have been great excitement when the family opened the parcels from their grandfather. Inside they found a bag of new potatoes, a sack of flour and a round of fresh, home-made cheese — more than enough to keep them going till their father returned from Hawick with more supplies. John's mum sat down and gathered the children round her to praise and thank God for his goodness to them in their time of need. Then, looking round at the eager faces of the hungry children she told them, 'O my children, love your heavenly Father. Tell him in

The High Street, Dumfries, about 1832
Reproduced by courtesy of Dumfries Museum

faith and prayer all your needs, and he will supply your wants
so far as it shall be for your good and his glory.'

John attended the village school until some time before his
twelfth birthday and was taught all the normal subjects offered
in schools in those days. Bible and Catechism studies occupied
an important place in the curriculum alongside English gram-
mar, history and geography and — especially important for
those who wanted to go on to university — mathematics, Latin
and Greek.

John had cause to remember one particular occasion when
he gained the top mark in Latin and expected to receive a prize,
but instead the prize was given to another pupil. He then began
to notice that it was usually the sons of wealthy parents who
gained prizes, whether they deserved them or not.

John was unhappy about this favouritism on the part of Mr
Smith, and wondered if it was worth working quite so hard at
his studies, but what he really could not stand was the teacher's
uncontrollable temper. One day in a fit of rage Mr Smith
subjected him to a severe flogging. John went home to his
mother and told her he was not going back to the school any
more, but when she begged him not to give up his schooling
he was eventually persaded to return. However, as soon as he
reappeared at school, Mr Smith attacked him a second time
and kicked him. That was the final straw for John. He rushed
out of the school and ran home, never to return. Even though
the teacher later came to the house and pleaded with him to go
back, he refused to do so.

John was sorry to leave school because he loved learning
and did well at his studies. Even at that young age he already
knew that when he grew up he wanted to go into the ministry,
or, better still, to go abroad as a missionary to some of the
heathen peoples for whom his father often prayed. He knew
that if he was to do so he needed a good education, but there
was no other school for him to go to and he had already

suffered enough at the hands (and feet!) of Mr Smith. There was no going back to that school!

So, although he was still under twelve years of age, John began work in his father's small stocking factory. Like the other workers, he had to work at the stocking frames from six in the morning till ten at night, with an hour off for lunch, half an hour for breakfast and another half-hour for tea. John used as much as possible of the little free time he had to study his books, especially Greek and Latin, which were important for anyone wanting to go into the ministry.

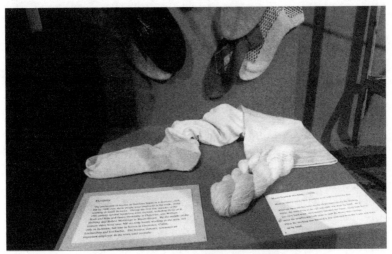

Traditional hand-framed woollen stockings
Photographedby courtesy of Dumfries Museum

At the time John may not have thought working at the stocking-making machines was a preparation for his dream of working on the missionfield, but he was later to thank God for the knowledge that he gained of machinery through this work, which was to prove a great help to him years later on the mission-field.

So we can see that even in the hard times and the disappointments, as well as in the love of his godly parents, who prayed for him and set him an example of humility and of a deep love for the Lord Jesus Christ, God was truly preparing John Paton for a great work on the foreign mission-field.

To think about

In this chapter we discover the love of the Paton family for the Lord's Day — it was the most important day of the week to that godly family. All Christians should love the first day of the week because it is the day we remember the resurrection of Christ. As the Paton family used that day for worship and praise of their God and Saviour, so also should all who love and serve the Lord Jesus Christ. It is a day when Christians can devote themselves to worship, prayer, reading the Scriptures and devotional books, visiting those who are in need and resting the body in preparation for the forthcoming week's work. If you say, 'What a bore!' then you are spiritually sick.

The islanders to whom John later took the gospel ignored the Lord's Day and at first treated it and the worship of God with contempt. But when they were converted they found the Lord's Day a true joy.

How do you spend the Lord's Day? What can you do to make this special day a joy to you and your family?

3.
Starting work

John was still keen to continue with his education, but in order to do this he needed money. Every penny he earned while working for his father at the stocking-frames was carefully saved until he had sufficient money to attend Dumfries Academy for six weeks. These few weeks in high school inspired John with a fresh desire for learning. He decided to look for some other type of work where he could earn more money so that he could continue with his studies at a higher level.

He first found a job with a government department who were undertaking a survey of the county of Dumfries in order to prepare detailed maps for the Ordinance Survey of Scotland. John's working day was now much shorter than it had been when he was working at his father's looms. He started work at 9 a.m. and finished at 4 p.m., though it was still a long day because he had to walk four miles each way to and from work.

In his lunch-hour, instead of playing football with the other lads, John would slip away to a quiet spot on the riverbank to read a book. One of the officials noticed him and eventually asked him what he was studying. John explained that he needed to continue his studies so that one day he could enter the ministry and become a missionary. The man went away and consulted his colleagues and this led to John's being

Dumfries Academy, the main entrance

offered a better job, with more pay and special training at the government's expense. At first, this must have seemed a wonderful opportunity to earn the money he needed to complete his education. However, when he was told that he would be required to sign up to work for seven years, John told his employer that he would be glad to work for three or four years (which would be all he needed to save enough money for his future schooling), but that seven years was too long.

The man couldn't believe his ears. 'Why?' he asked in amazement. 'Will you refuse an offer that many gentlemen's sons would be proud of?'

John explained: 'My life is given to another Master, so I cannot engage for seven years.'

The official asked sharply who this master was. When John answered that it was the Lord Jesus and went on to say, 'I want to prepare as soon as possible for his service in the proclaiming of the gospel,' the man was very angry. He rushed to the door and called in the officer responsible for paying the lads their wages, shouting as he did so, 'Accept my offer, or you are dismissed on the spot!'

When John repeated that he could not commit himself for as long as seven years the man refused to listen any more and dismissed him at once.

When the rector, or principal, of Dumfries Academy heard of John's dismissal he was so shocked at what had happened that he offered to let him attend classes there free of charge. But John felt he could not accept, because he did not want to be a burden on his parents. Indeed, as the oldest son, he wanted to contribute to the family income and help with the expenses of the younger children's education.

He therefore made his way to the hiring fair at Lockerbie, where young men and women would go when they were looking for a job. There he found work on a farm as a temporary labourer during the harvest. The first time he tried to tie the corn into a bundle, or sheaf, it all fell to pieces as soon as the farmer picked it up! But the farmer was a kind man, who soon showed him how to tie a bundle that would not split open even when it was tossed across the field. As well as helping with the harvest, John dug and planted a garden near the house for the farmer's wife. It was hard work, but all that he learned about farming and gardening was one day to prove invaluable on the mission-field.

In the meantime John had applied for a job in Glasgow with the Reformed Presbyterian Church in West Campbell Street. They wanted a young man to visit homes in the area, especially those of children who had at one time attended the Sunday School, and also to distribute gospel tracts. As well as a salary of £50 a year, the successful candidate would have a year's free training in a seminary, which would qualify him to teach in a school and be a big step towards entering the Christian ministry. John was one of two candidates invited to attend for an interview and examination.

When the day came, he wrapped his few belongings in his handkerchief and set out for Glasgow. He had to walk the first forty miles, and then catch a train for the rest of the journey. John's father accompanied him for the first few miles. As they walked together, his father encouraged him to remain loyal to his faithful God, but as they approached the spot where they had to part, he grew silent and his lips moved silently as he prayed to God for his son.

When it was time for John's dad to turn back, he gripped his son firmly by the hand and with tears in his eyes bade him farewell with the words: 'God bless you, my son! Your father's God prosper you and keep you from all evil!' Then after a few more moments of silent prayer, in which they were both too overcome to speak, his dad gave him a big hug and John ran on his way. But he had not gone very far before he stopped to look back for one last view of the father whom he

The Broomiehall, Glasgow, early nineteenth century.

loved so dearly and he caught sight of his dad doing exactly the same thing.

John found the parting with his parents and brothers and sisters heartbreaking, for they were a close family, and as he was himself to say in later years, 'stuck to each other and the old folks like burs'. As he lost sight of his father in the distance, he made a silent promise in his heart that, with God's help, he would always 'live and act so as never to grieve or dishonour such a father and mother as he had given me'.

When John arrived in Glasgow for the interview, the examiners could not decide between the two applicants, so they eventually offered the job to both. This meant that they would not only share the work between them (which gave them more time to study), but that the salary of £50 a year, that had originally been intended to support just one employee, was also divided between them.

The two lads got on very well together, but they found it hard work, especially as the other students were all well ahead of them in their studies. The long hours and the lack of good food led to them both having a breakdown in health, so that they were forced to give up the work before the year was over. John, who had a troublesome cough that could have been a symptom of a serious lung disease, was ordered home by the local doctor. However, after a few weeks of spending time in the open air, as well as enjoying his mother's good home cooking and drinking plenty of fresh milk from the family cow, he was soon well enough to be thinking of finding work again.

He next tried his hand at schoolteaching in a small school at a place called Girvan, but when he had managed to save £10 out of his earnings he gave up the job and returned to his studies at college in Glasgow. However, even in those days £10 did not last long and all too soon John once again found himself forced to look for work. He was so short of money that he even thought about selling his books, but he could not pluck up the courage to go into the shop with them. Thinking people were watching him suspiciously as he stood outside hesitating, he ran off in alarm, afraid of being taken for a thief. He wandered about for some time, not knowing where he was going, until a notice in a window caught his eye. It was an advertisement for the post of teacher at the Maryhill Free Church School. A bus was just passing, going in that direction, so he jumped on it and went straight off to see about the job. He realized afterwards that, even when he was walking aimlessly through the streets, God had been guiding him, so that he would see that notice and get the job.

John was to show something of the strength of character in his new work that was to fit him so well for work on the missionfield. The school where he was now teaching was situated in a tough area of Glasgow. The three previous teachers had all been forced to leave because of difficulties with discipline and the terrible behaviour of some of the students.

As well as the boys and girls who attended the school during the day, there were evening classes for older students. Many of those who attended these classes worked in the mills and coalmines during the daytime. They were tough young people who had no respect for a schoolteacher. When John took up the post, the minister handed him a heavy cane and told him, 'Use that freely, or you will never keep order here.' John replied that he would only use the cane as a last resort, as he hoped to be able to keep order by other means.

However, only a few days later he was confronted by a rough young man and woman who deliberately set out to disrupt the lesson by talking and laughing all the time. When John warned the couple to be quiet they ignored him and went on making more noise and making the other pupils laugh. Finally, John told the young man to leave if he would not behave properly. At that the young fellow leapt to his feet and began squaring up to John, ready for a fight.

John quietly picked up the key, walked to the door of the classroom and locked it, putting the key in his pocket. Then he warned the rest of the class not to interfere as he picked up the cane and began to hit the young man with it. The lad tried to strike out at him with his fists, but John was agile and managed to keep out of his way while all the time continuing to rain blows on him with the cane.

Eventually the young man was exhausted and gave up the fight. John sent him back to his desk and the rest of the class were strangely quiet as he went on to warn them that trouble-makers had better stay away in future. He made it clear that he would prefer not to have to use the cane and, though he had to threaten to use it on one or two more occasions, the pupils soon settled down to their studies. Before long John was able to put the cane away for good. He found the students responded well to his methods of giving praise when they did well and expressing his disappointment in them when their work was done badly.

The school did so well with John in charge that its reputation began to spread throughout the city and the number of students attending grew steadily. But after a time the school committee decided that, as the school was doing so well, they could afford to appoint a teacher with higher academic qualifications. So once again John found himself looking for a job. As he took his problem to God, seeking guidance, he could not help feeling sad about leaving his pupils. He was uncertain of what the future held for him, but knew that God would be glorified in whatever was to happen.

To think about

John, from his younger days, saw great value in education. He knew that in order to achieve his goals, he needed the best education possible. The same is true today — if we would best serve the Lord we need to be educated. We must be able to read before the Bible becomes a readable book. If you would be a missionary there are many skills you need to make your work a success — God will use your skills to his glory in the salvation of sinners.

John had the opportunity to take up a well-paid job, but he was not concerned about material possessions: all he wanted was for sinners to come to faith in Christ.

Today it is not just young people who are involved in study. I know many people who took up studies late in life. Now what is the purpose of your education? As you plan your future do you take into consideration how best you can serve Christ with the education you undertake?

4.
The Glasgow City Mission

John did not have to wait long for the guidance for which he had prayed. Some time previously he had applied to the Glasgow City Mission for a post as one of their workers. The very night before he was due to leave Maryhill School, he received a letter from the mission asking him to appear before a committee who were to examine him to see if he was qualified for missionary work in a needy part of that great city.

The interviewing committee not only spent time questioning John about his knowledge of the Christian faith, but also took him to visit the homes of some of the poorer families in the city where he spoke to them about the saving work of the Lord Jesus. The mission committee wanted to see how John got on with people. It would be no use giving such important work to someone who could not work well with all kinds of people. Then he had to preach a sermon in front of a congregation which included the examiners.

It all happened so quickly that John did not have a lot of time to prepare and hardly dared to hope that he would make a good impression. However, with the Lord's help all went well and a few days later he was told that he had been accepted as one of the City Missionaries.

John's job was not an easy one. He was expected to spend four hours each day, from Monday to Saturday, going from door to door, visiting homes and holding Bible studies and prayer meetings in any homes where the family were willing for him to do so. There would also be meetings in the evenings with a special evangelistic service each Sunday evening. The only place he could find to hold them was in a hayloft over a barn where a number of cows were kept. To get to the meetings the congregation had to climb up a rickety wooden staircase on the outside of the building.

At first the work was slow and the numbers attending the meetings were very few, but when John told his congregation that the mission directors were thinking of moving him to another part of the city if numbers did not increase, they made an effort to invite along more people. John's people were afraid of losing him!

As the work grew, with meetings for different groups being held every day of the week, John gathered a band of workers about him who helped take the gospel to the unsaved. Among other things, he was responsible for weekly Bible classes, catechism classes, singing classes and a communicants' class which prepared people for membership in one of the local churches.

The Lord's Day began with a Bible Class at 7 a.m. In the early days John used to set out every Sunday morning at 6 a.m. He then spent an hour running from one house to another, knocking on the doors to wake people up ready for the class. (Later, when the class was established, some of the young people themselves took over the job of rounding up those who might not otherwise have arrived on time.) Between seventy and a hundred young people from some of the poorest homes in the city used to attend this class. They were dressed in their ordinary, everyday working clothes, since they had nothing else to wear. Many of them did not even have any shoes. But as people were converted to faith in Christ they began to work harder and no longer wasted their money on drink. John

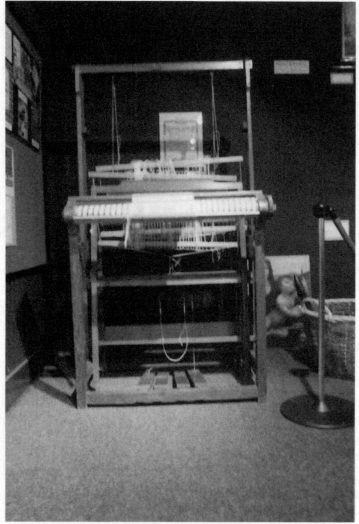

Weaving loom
Photographed by courtesy of Dumfries Museum

John mentions weavers in Torthorwald in his boyhood. Many of those who attended his Bible classes in Glasgow would also have worked in the textile-weaving industry, though most were probably employed in factories where they would have operated larger looms than this one.

noticed that they began to take more trouble with their appearance, and it was not long before they came along wearing a pair of shoes. Then, bit by bit as they could afford it, other new clothes appeared. However, some still continued to wear their old clothes although they could afford better ones, in order to make newcomers feel at home when they attended services dressed in their working clothes.

By now, the Sunday services had moved out of the hayloft over the cowshed as the mission had been able to buy a group of buildings. They had turned one of the buildings into a church and beside it they founded a school for poor boys and girls in the neighbourhood. A teacher was employed for the school and the ladies in John's congregation helped to supply clothes, books and even food for the children, many of whom would otherwise have had to wear ragged clothes and did not get enough to eat at home.

In addition to all these meetings, John was still expected to spend at least four hours a day in visiting homes. He was often kept busy for up to eight hours at a time, going from one house to another and spending time with people, talking with them about the Lord Jesus. Some of the young men and women used to help him by going round the homes with tracts, but whenever John heard that anyone was ill, or in special need of help, he always made a point of going to see the person himself.

Many of the problems in this part of Glasgow had been caused through drunkenness, and John was very active in promoting the cause of 'total abstinence' — that is, in encouraging people to give up drinking alcohol altogether, because of all the harm it caused.

One of the homes where he held meetings in the early days belonged to an Irishwoman, whose husband was a drunkard. He used to spend all the family's hard-earned money on drink and even to beat his wife when he came home after a bout of drinking. In time, however, as a result of the witness and prayers of the man's wife and of the group who met regularly in his home, this man came to hear the gospel and was saved. Turning from his sinful ways, he became a faithful servant of the God who loved him. He not only gave up drinking, but was very active in urging others to do the same, as well as inviting outsiders along to the meetings.

John and other Christians used to hold public meetings in the open air at which they preached the gospel and proclaimed Christ as the one who could save drunkards from their life of slavery to alcoholic drink and make them new people, who would love and serve God. In order to be easily seen, John, or another preacher, would stand at the top of a flight of outside steps which led up to the second floor of one of the houses, while a group of other Christians gathered round to listen. The men would take turns at preaching. Some of the people from the mission would sing a few rousing hymns, and before long a good crowd would have gathered.

As a result of the work of John and the other Christians, more and more men and women turned away from their drinking and the sinful behaviour which this caused. This alarmed the owners of the public houses, because they were losing many of their customers and were no longer making so much money. Some of the publicans started going along to the public meetings in order to heckle and disrupt them.

On one occasion the publicans tried to get the police to stop the meetings. The police officer in charge, who was himself a Christian, agreed to send some of his men along to keep an eye on the proceedings, but refused to stop the meeting unless there really was trouble. When it became known that the police would be there to break up the meeting and arrest troublemakers, an even larger crowd than usual gathered, thinking they would watch the fun.

When the time for the meeting came, a number of police officers mingled with the crowd. During the singing of the first hymn the police captain climbed the stairs to the platform, where he joined the leaders and everyone could see that he was listening quietly to all that was said. With all the police officers present, no one dared cause any trouble. The men who had complained were too embarrassed to slip away, when it was they who had asked the police along in the first place, so they too were forced to stay and listen to the preaching! Far from succeeding in putting a stop to the meetings, they had actually helped John and his companions by giving them more publicity!

Of course, many of the police were sympathetic to the work John was doing, because they saw that their work was made a lot easier when drunkards were converted. Also, a number of them knew John Paton personally because they attended the prayer meetings which he held for police officers when they came off duty.

The publicans were furious when they found that their plan to have the police stop the meetings had backfired, so they decided to get their own back on John and his friends. During one of the services, they put a cart across the entrance to the church, completely blocking it, so that no one could get out of the building when the meeting was over.

When John sent a couple of young men to move the cart out of the way they were arrested and marched off to the police station. John ran after them, but the policemen on duty that day were on the side of the publicans and he too was taken along to the police station. When they arrived there, it seemed as if the publicans had won the day. The officer in charge wrote down a note of all the complaints against the Christians, but refused to listen when John and his friends tried to put their side of the case. It really looked as if the police were going to lay charges against them.

Suddenly a well-dressed man, who was obviously someone important, stepped forward, and offered to stand bail for the men. A short, sharp discussion followed with the police officers, and the man told them, 'I know this whole case, I will expose it to the bottom; expect me here to stand by the missionary and these young men on Monday morning.' With that, he walked out of the police station before John was able to thank him for his help. Then the police officer came over to John and his companions and politely told them that the charges were being withdrawn and they were free to go. John never found out who the man was. However, we can be sure that God was watching over his servants, and that he sent the man along at just the right time to stop them from being locked up or taken to court.

One of the men that John used to visit was a very good doctor, but he had a serious drink problem which caused him and his family a lot of unhappiness. After talking with this man for a long time and reading the Bible to him, John asked him, 'Shall we pray?' The man told him that not only he *did* not pray, but that he *could* not pray — only curse. John, however, would not give up and, putting his hands on the man's shoulders to keep him down on his knees, prayed for him, pleading with God to have mercy on him.

The next time John came to see him, the man came hurrying to meet him, threw his arms around him and exclaimed, 'Thank God, I can pray now!' Everything had changed! That morning, for the first time in his life, he had prayed with his wife and children and, he said, from then on he would do so every day. He gave up his drinking, joined a church and began to witness to his patients about the Lord Jesus, who had saved him from a life of sin. When John and his friends heard of people who were ill, but too poor to pay for a doctor to see them, they would send them to this man, who was glad to treat them free of charge, out of love for the Lord.

John also set aside time to work amongst those who openly hated Christianity. Here again we see something of his strength of character. He took every opportunity to explain the gospel to them. Sometimes he had vigorous debates with groups of young men about the truths of Christianity. At other times he visited people in their homes and spent long hours talking to them and praying with them.

One man was ill and thought he was dying. He was terrified of death. The prospect of facing the God he had mocked filled him with dread. However, John was able to visit him and explain the gospel to him. As he heard the message of forgiveness in Christ, the man shed tears over his sins and cried out to God to save him.

This man had a large collection of books, which he used to lend out to other people. These were all books which contained false teaching, against the truths of the Bible. Though he had often spoken against the Bible and made fun of it, he had never actually read it for himself, or understood its teaching.

When John gave him a Bible he was delighted to receive it, exclaiming, 'This is the book for me now!' He went on to tell John that, since they last met, he had collected together his library of evil books in one room. His wife had locked the door, so that no one could disturb them. Then his wife and daughter had torn all the books to pieces and the family had made a big bonfire of them.

Sadly, not all of those whom John tried to help were converted. One man who was dying was in terrible pain. He wanted nothing to do with God or the gospel, but his wife begged the missionary to visit him, which John eventually agreed to do.

When John came to see him, the man refused to listen to what he had to say, and even spat at him when he tried to speak to him about the Lord Jesus. When John offered to pray with him, the man told him to pray to the devil for him. John was horrified, but did not think the man really meant what he said. 'Yes,' the man shouted, 'I believe there is a devil, and a God, and a just God, too; but I have hated him in life, and I hate him in death.' And so he died, with those terrible words of hate upon his lips.

A number of people who lived in the district where John worked were Roman Catholics. Some welcomed him into their homes and allowed him to read the Scriptures and pray with them.

One young Roman Catholic woman was converted as a result of going to John's meetings and Bible Classes. She went to live with a Protestant family, but one night a group of Catholics drove up to the door of the house in a closed carriage and tried to kidnap the girl and her little sister and take them to a convent. The girl, who was ill in bed at the time, refused to go with them and her friends sent for John. By the time he arrived the house was full of people, all shouting and arguing. After a struggle, during which the poor young woman fainted, John managed to get away. He was able to grab the key to the house-door and locked them all in while he ran to the police to get help.

However, the two policemen who came to the house to see what was going on were themselves Roman Catholics and instead of freeing the girl and arresting the kidnappers, as John had hoped, they actually helped the kidnappers by clearing a way through the crowd for them as they forcefully carried the struggling girl to the carriage.

A gentleman in the crowd took John's part and warned one of the policemen in the street outside not to let the carriage get away. The policeman, who was a big, strong man, pulled out his truncheon and aimed a blow at the driver as he was lashing at the horses to get them to pull away. At that, the driver jumped down to avoid being hit, flinging the reins in the policeman's face. The policeman promptly leapt up into the

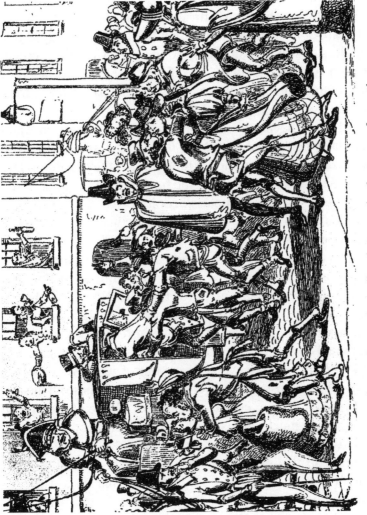

Glasgow roughs causing a disturbance at the departure of a coach

driver's empty seat and drove the carriage to the police station. However, when they arrived there it was discovered that the kidnappers had somehow managed to escape.

Then, to make matters worse, it turned out that the officer in charge that evening was himself a Roman Catholic. After he had heard both sides of the argument he let the carriage leave, with the girl still held inside by some of the Catholic women. Turning to John he said, 'Her friends are taking her to a comfortable home; you have no right to interfere, and I have let them go.'

Although the mission authorities later took up the case and eventually persuaded the police that the girl really had been abducted and that they should look for her, they could find no trace of her. Some time later, she turned up at the door of the poorhouse — where homeless people who had nowhere else to go could find shelter — but by then she was very ill and she died soon afterwards.

After this incident, John received a number of threatening letters and more than once things were thrown at him, especially in areas where many of the Irish Roman Catholics lived. Once he was struck by a stone which knocked him down and gave him a nasty cut just above his eye. By the time he scrambled to his feet no one was to be seen! At other times pails of boiling water were tipped out of windows or down flights of stairs just as he was going by, though these all missed their mark and John escaped unscathed. Some of the priests hated him so much for his work among their people that they publicly cursed him in their church services.

When all this was going on, the directors of the mission thought it might be wise if John left the area for a while, to allow tempers to cool. They suggested that he take a holiday, or even that he should be transferred to Edinburgh for a year. But John Paton was a brave man. He believed that with God's help he could stand up to the enemies of the cross and win the victory. So, refusing to leave his people, he carried on with his work as usual.

At about this time John, who had been working as a missionary in Glasgow for several years, was elected to serve as an elder in the church there.

John's work in Glasgow lasted for ten years. During that time his labours were greatly blessed by God. He not only saw a steady increase in the numbers attending his meetings and classes, but also evidence of a true growth in godliness among those who professed faith in Christ.

In time many of the converts were able to afford a better standard of living and moved to other parts of the town. When this happened John kept in contact with them until they were settled in a local church. In later years when John went to address any church in Glasgow about his missionary work he would be sure to find someone in the congregation who had once been a member of his Bible Class.

All this time too, he continued with his studies — first at the University of Glasgow and later at a Bible College called the Reformed Presbyterian Divinity Hall. He also attended medical classes at the Andersonian College. It was hard work and his long hours of holding meetings and visiting people left him little time for study, but he never lost the vision of one day going to serve the Lord overseas and he was anxious to be properly qualified as a preacher of the gospel.

To think about

John worked very hard during his time in Glasgow. The reason for this was to serve the Lord the best he could. Then as hardened sinners turned to Christ he noticed that their standard of living improved. This has happened in many parts of the world where Christ has been preached and people converted. The same happens today.

John found that people began to read their Bibles, attend worship, give up drinking and look after their families when Christ became their Lord and Saviour. Have you seen any changes in people you know who have come to faith in Christ?

John's work was hated by the owners of public houses, the Roman Catholics and other groups. Why do people hate Christ and those who serve him?

5.
Preparing for the mission-field

John was happy in his work in Glasow and knew the Lord was blessing him in it, but ever since he was a boy he had longed to serve Christ on the overseas mission-field. He had always had a special interest in the heathen people of the South Sea Islands, most of whom had never heard of the true God and his Son, the Lord Jesus Christ, who had come into the world to save sinners. As John went about his duties it seemed to him that he could hear the pitiful cries of those poor people, dying without a knowledge of the Saviour, and he longed to be able to go and help them. He did not tell anyone what he was thinking, but he prayed about it a lot and this was why he had begun to study medicine as well as theology.

A missionary from the church to which John belonged, the Rev. John Inglis, had already been working for some years in the islands of the New Hebrides in the South Pacific (now called Vanuatu). This man needed helpers and the church officers in Scotland appealed for volunteers to go out and join him in his work, but no one came forward. At a meeting of the Synod of the Reformed Presbyterian Church of Scotland, at which John was present, each delegate was asked to write down on a piece of paper the names of three men he considered suitable for missionary work among the islanders of the South

Pacific. The papers were then collected and counted to see if anyone had the confidence of the majority of those present.

John waited with the others in a hushed silence while the papers were being examined, and tears sprang to his eyes when he heard that no one had been chosen. He felt like jumping up from his seat and calling out: 'Here am I. Send me!' But, as he wanted to be really sure that it was the Lord who was calling him, he waited and thought and prayed about it for a few more days. At last he went to see the leader of the committee responsible for the mission to the New Hebrides and offered himself as a missionary.

When he returned to his lodgings, he made a joke about what he had just done, telling his friend and fellow student, Joseph Copeland, 'I have been away signing my banishment. I have offered myself as a missionary for the New Hebrides.'

Joseph did not reply at once, but after a while, to John's great surprise, he said that if the mission committee would accept him, he too would go.

After interviews, both men were accepted for the work, subject to their passing the usual examinations for men entering the ministry. They also had to spend a year learning basic medicine and gaining other skills which would be useful to them when they were living far away from civilization.

John's parents were truly delighted when they heard the news. Only then did they tell him that ever since he was born they had been praying that one day he would become a missionary. They had not told him before as they had not wanted to put pressure on him, but wanted to be sure it was really the Lord who had called him to this work. But now they wanted him to know that they, and indeed all his family, would be praying that God would give him great success in the work he was about to undertake and that he would live to see many of the South Sea islanders brought to know and love the Saviour.

It was a good thing that John knew he had the support of his family, because when he told the people in Glasgow of his decision he met with a great deal of opposition.

Many people told him that the work he was doing in Glasgow was just as important as missionary work overseas and that, as he had a work to do there in the city, he should not leave it, as one old man put it, to 'throw away his life amongst cannibals'.

John was genuinely concerned about the work he would be leaving behind, but he thought there were many other people who could take it over if he left. On the other hand, there was no one else, it seemed, to go to the people of the New Hebrides if he did not!

Often when people told John that there were plenty of 'heathens at home', and that he was needed to work amongst them, he felt that these men and women were not really sincere in their concern for the needy people at home since they made no attempt to help them themselves. In fact he thought they would spend ten times as much on themselves in one day (on expensive clothes, or a meal out, for example) as they would give to missionary work — at home or abroad — in the course of a whole year.

Another time an old Christian tried to discourage him from going by warning him, 'The cannibals! You will be eaten by cannibals!'

John replied by reminding him that he himself was an old man, who could expect to die soon, and to be laid in the grave, where his body would be eaten by worms. John then went on: 'If I can but live and die serving and honouring the Lord Jesus, it will make no difference to me whether I am eaten by cannibals or by worms; and in the Great Day my resurrection body will arise as fair as yours in the likeness of our risen Redeemer.'

At that, the old gentleman threw up his hands in despair and walked out of the room with the words: 'After that I have nothing more to say!'

John was not afraid of dying. After all, he knew that, like everyone, he would have to die sooner or later, and he could only die once. He was quite content to leave the time, place and manner of his death in the hands of his God. Besides he had often risked his life during his work in Glasgow, when he had visited the homes of people suffering from cholera and other deadly diseases.

Eventually the problem of who was to take over John's work in Glasgow was solved when his younger brother Walter gave up a good, well-paid job to join the Glasgow City Mission and carry on the work there in John's place. Now John could devote all his energies to preparing for his future work in the New Hebrides!

During all the years John had been working in Glasgow he had always saved out of his hard-earned wages as much money as he possibly could to send to his parents, to help them meet the expenses of bringing up his younger brothers and sisters. First, he had been able to help them buy a cow and pay for the right for it to graze on Bank Hill. He had also helped with the rent of their house and the costs of schooling for the younger children.

Then the family found themselves having to take out a very large loan to pay off the arrears of rent on his grandfather's cottage, when a new owner suddenly demanded payment of a sum going back for several years, which his grandfather had never expected to have to pay. The old man could not pay it all back himself and John's father, and later John himself, had taken on the responsibility for payment of the debt. When John received his first salary from the mission, to allow him to buy what he needed for going overseas, he was thrilled to be able to send home enough money to pay off the rest of that debt. So

Plaque commemorating John G. Paton's association with the South
Seas, entrance to Torthorwald churchyard.

Paton family grave, Torthorwald churchyard (for the inscription see
p.185). In the surrounding fields cattle and sheep graze on the slopes
above the village, much as they did in John's day.

he was able to leave knowing that his parents no longer had that worry hanging over them.

He was also very thankful to know that he was leaving behind his younger brothers and sisters who would take good care of his parents as they grew older and see that they would not lack any comfort in their old age.

John and his friend Joseph Copeland both passed their examinations and were formally 'licensed' to preach the gospel on 1 December 1857. They then spent four months travelling the length and breadth of Scotland visiting churches and Sunday Schools to tell people about the work they were going to do and asking for their prayers and support in the years ahead. Finally, on 23 March 1858 a special service was held at John's church in Glasgow at which they were both ordained as ministers of the gospel and formally commissioned, or 'set apart', to serve the Lord as missionaries to the New Hebrides.

In the meantime the young people of John's mission clubbed together to buy rolls of material which they made up into dresses, kilts and trousers for John and Joseph to take with them for the men and women of the New Hebrides. Long after John had left for the mission-field they continued to make up parcels of clothing and send them out to him. Whenever he opened one of these packages he would think of the friends back at home who had made all the clothes and many of whom had, at some time or another, been members of one of his Bible Classes.

To think about

John believed he was 'called' to be a missionary to the people of the South Sea islands who had never heard the gospel and he devoted his time and energy towards this end.

He left Great Britain and went to the New Hebrides. Some people rejoiced to know of John's decision, while others tried to talk him out of what they believed to be a foolish decision. There were many people who supported John in a variety of ways all the time he worked on the mission-field.

Maybe some reader feels led to serve the Lord in a special way. You must find out all you can about the work you believe you want to do, then look at your skills and family situation and pray for spiritual wisdom in order to come to a wise decision.

Some people I know post a large parcel of spectacles to missionaries in South Africa. These old glasses are very useful to people who cannot afford to buy new ones. How can you assist the missionaries in foreign lands?

6.
The New Hebrides at last!

On 16 April 1858 John and his friend Joseph Copeland set sail from the port of Greenock on the ship *Clutha*, bound for Australia, on the first stage of their journey to the New Hebrides. With them, as they stood on the deck watching the coast of Scotland slip away, was John's wife Mary, whom he had recently married.

Mary Ann Paton (whose surname before she was married was Robson) had grown up in a Christian home and from an early age had truly loved the Lord. She was a bright girl and, in days when girls did not always go to school, her parents made sure she had a good education. Like her husband, she was enthusiastic about missionary work and looked forward to telling the women and boys and girls of the New Hebrides about the Saviour.

The voyage to Australia took a long time, but was uneventful. The captain of the ship was a Christian who held regular services on board and encouraged John to take Bible Classes among the crew and passengers.

When they reached Australia, John and his wife Mary landed at Melbourne and spent a few days with some missionaries who lived there. Joseph stayed on board ship to look after their boxes and the two small boats they were taking with them to the islands. He also made enquiries among the other ships at the docks for one to take them on to the New Hebrides. Eventually he found the captain of an American vessel, the *Francis P. Sage*, who agreed to drop the missionaries and their luggage off at Aneityum, one of the southern islands in the New Hebrides group, as the ship sailed past on its way to Penang.

It only took twelve days to sail from Melbourne to Aneityum but it seemed a long time to the missionaries as on this ship everything was very noisy, with a lot of shouting and swearing from the crew. The captain boasted that he employed the second mate to swear at the crew and knock them about. The ship anchored ten miles off the coast of Aneityum and the captain refused to go in any closer to the shore. The missionaries wondered if this was because he treated the sailors so badly that he was afraid that if they went near enough for the long-suffering crew to land they would have all deserted the ship and refused to come back on board!

Eventually a boat came out from the island to find out what they wanted and John was able to send a note to the missionaries who were already working on this island. Soon afterwards two mission boats, the *John Knox* and the *Colombia*, arrived on the scene and the three missionaries with all their belongings were transferred to them from the ship.

All the small boats were piled high and when it was time to sail John, Mary and two of the local missionaries had to clamber on top of a pile of boxes on board the *John Knox* and hold on tight. As their boat turned to move off towards the shore its mast accidentally struck a small crane on the side of ship and snapped off. John grabbed hold of Mary and dragged her out of the way just in time as the mast crashed to the deck. If he had not acted so quickly she would almost certainly have been killed.

Without a mast, their boat was drifting helplessly. The captain of the American ship just sailed away and left them to it, but some of the mission boats managed to take the *John Knox* in tow, and with a lot of hard rowing they eventually made it safely to land.

John Paton and his party finally stepped ashore on the soil of the New Hebrides on the evening of 30 August 1858, four and a half months after leaving Scotland. They were warmly welcomed by all the missionaries and their wives and by a number of the local people who had become Christians through the work of these missionaries. Together they all gave thanks to God for bringing John, Mary and Joseph safely to these islands.

The next few weeks were busy ones as the men were helping the other missionaries with building work while Mary spent time with the other missionary wives learning about life on the islands. This building experience was to prove invaluable later when John had to construct mission compound buildings.

One of the first things they all did was to get together and discuss the best place for the newcomers to start their work. Two missionaries from Canada, Mr and Mrs Mathieson, were already working at Kwamera on the southern side of an island called Tanna. It was soon decided that John and Mary would also settle on that island, but they would live in the north at Port Resolution. Joseph Copeland would move between the two couples to help them both as he was needed. To begin with, he spent most of his time sailing between Aneityum and Tanna on the *John Knox,* helping the captain to transport timber and other building materials needed for building homes for the missionaries as well as a church building.

Before they could start building they had first to buy a plot of land from the natives. They also had to pay the natives to burn lime in kilns to make plaster for the walls and to plait sugar-cane leaves together to make thatch for the roof. All this meant a lot of hard bargaining. The missionaries paid for the land and the materials they needed for their building work, not with money, which would have been of no use to the natives, with their primitive way of life, but with axes, knives, fishhooks, blankets and clothing.

The chiefs from whom the missionaries bought the land to build their house proved to be very crafty and they were later to demand several more payments, threatening the missionaries with death if they dared to touch any of the trees or build a fence. If the missionaries handed over more knives or clothing, all would be well for a time, but then the demands would start all over again.

What the missionaries did not know, and no one told them until it was too late, was that both the sites chosen for their homes were in very unhealthy spots, because they were too close to the shore and the air was always very moist and still, with no breeze. This meant that there were a lot of mosquitoes and the area was a breeding-ground for malaria and other fevers. These diseases posed a constant threat to the missionaries, who were not used to such a climate. It was only much later that one of the local chiefs was to tell John, 'Missi, if you stay here, you will soon die! No Tanna-man sleeps so low down as you do, in this damp weather, or he too would die. We sleep on the high ground, and the trade-wind keeps us well…'

However it was there, in a sheltered spot at the foot of a hill, close to the shore of a beautiful bay surrounded by palm trees, that the Patons made their first home and began their work among the dreaded cannibals of the South Seas.

A sea-going man, who had travelled widely, once described the chiefs on the island of Tanna as 'the ugliest, the most indecent, the most grotesque, and the most utterly barbarous both in appearance and actual fact, of any people whom we have yet seen'.[1] These were the people among whom John and Mary had come to work.

---

1. R. Ward (ed.), *Presbyterian Leaders in Nineteenth Century Australia*, Aust. Print Group, Melbourne, 1993, p.123.

To think about

Reading the story of John Paton and his intention to take the gospel to a people who were known to be cannibals, I wonder if he was wise to take a wife with him. The apostle Paul said he had every right to be married (1 Corinthians 9:5), but on another occasion that it was unwise to marry (1 Corinthians 7:25-40). Both John and Mary were willing to make great sacrifices in the service they rendered to Christ — and that is the important matter.

Today we find some teachers telling us that as God loves everyone and all will one day get to heaven, missionary effort is not required. Is this a true biblical doctrine? Is it possible for people to be saved if they have no saving knowledge of Christ?

7.
A taste of the cannibals

When John first saw the natives of Tanna, his heart sank. The men were all naked, with their faces painted in bright colours, especially when they were preparing for battle. Sometimes they would paint one cheek red and the other black, or they would have white eyebrows and a blue chin. In their hair they wore feathers, which stuck out at all angles, and they always carried spears and clubs, ready to attack anyone who offended them. The women wore short grass skirts, while the young girls often wore long strings of beads round their necks and crude earrings made from tortoiseshell.

John thought of the people he had left behind in Glasgow and just for a moment he wondered if he had done the right thing in leaving them to come to work among such savage people. But then he remembered the Christian islanders whom he had met on Aneityum and the big change that God had brought about in their lives. This encouraged him and Mary to hope and pray that God would do the same thing on the island of Tanna.

It was in fact only some twenty years earlier that the very first Christian missionaries had come to the New Hebrides. In November 1839 two British missionaries, John Williams and James Harris, had set foot on the nearby island of Erromanga. No sooner had they landed than they were clubbed to death and their bodies cooked and eaten!

John Williams on the LMS ship *Camden*, 1839

The next missionaries to arrive, George Turner and Henry Nisbet, had actually settled on Tanna, but within a few months they had to flee for their lives. They made their escape at night, using a small boat, and were eventually rescued by a whaling-ship which called in at the islands. They landed in Samoa and stayed there for many years, working among the people of those islands instead.

Over the years a number of missionaries were sent from Samoa to the New Hebrides, but none of them stayed long, because of the illnesses they suffered as a result of the unhealthy climate, as well as the cruel treatment they received from the natives.

Dr George Turner, missionary on Tanna 1842-43 and later head of
Malua Training Institution, Samoa

Mission house at Port Resolution, Tanna, which was the home of
George Turner and Henry Nisbet and their wives during their short stay
on the island

At last, in 1848, Dr John Geddie and his wife settled on Aneityum, the southernmost island in the group. Four years later, in 1852, they were joined by a Scottish couple, Dr John Inglis and his wife, who began work on the other side of the island. These were the missionaries who had welcomed John, Mary and Joseph on their arrival and helped them to get started in their own work.

God greatly blessed the labours of these missionaries and within a few years around 3,500 natives had thrown away their dead idols of wood and stone and begun worshipping the living God of the Bible, trusting in the Lord Jesus for salvation. Family worship was introduced into the homes and before each meal the islanders would give thanks to God for providing their daily needs.

Christian chief from Aneityum

The missionaries also began the work of translating the Bible into the language of the islanders. This was a task on which Joseph Copeland was to spend many long hours in the years ahead. The printing of the Bible was to be a very costly undertaking and it was the islanders themselves who found a way to raise the money for this project. A portion of the land used for growing crops was set apart for growing arrowroot, which they carefully tended. The arrowroot was sold to traders from overseas, who valued it for its very high quality compared with that grown in other countries.

Every penny which the islanders received from the sale of the arrowroot over fifteen years was carefully saved and put towards the cost of printing and publishing the precious Word of the living God.

Meanwhile, back on the island of Tanna, there was a lot of coming and going among the native warriors, all of whom were in a state of great excitement, and John soon learnt that war was in the air. The local chiefs had promised the missionaries when they bought the land that they would not harm them, but added that they could make no promises about what the other tribes might do if there was a war. In fact, John soon realized that such promises really meant nothing at all!

One day a fight broke out between men from two different tribes. The missionaries were alarmed to see all the armed warriors rushing past, uttering blood-curdling yells, and to hear gunshots coming from among the trees.

Some of the native women grabbed their children and rushed off to find somewhere safe to shelter while the fighting was going on, but others just stayed around chewing on pieces of sugar-cane, talking and laughing among themselves as if nothing unusual was going on. Obviously fights with other tribes were just part of everyday life for them!

The missionaries heard later that five or six warriors had been killed in the fighting. The victorious tribesmen carried the bodies of the victims to a spot less than a mile from where John and Mary's home was being built. There, beside a spring of fresh water, they cooked the bodies of their enemies and ate them.

The next morning when a young lad from Aneityum, who was working as a cook for the missionaries, went to the spring to fetch some water to make tea, he was gone much longer than usual. Finally, he returned with an empty can. He was very upset and worried. 'Missi,' he said, using the name which the islanders always used to address the missionaries, 'this is a

dark land. The people of this land do dark works. At the boiling
spring they have cooked and feasted upon the slain. They have
washed the blood into the water; they have bathed there,
polluting everything. I cannot get pure water to make your tea.
What shall I do?'

The boy was very relieved when Dr Inglis told him they
would drink coconut juice instead until he could find pure
water. However, what really struck John was the fact that the
lad was far more concerned about the pollution of the water
than about the warriors killing and eating other men.

That night, as the missionaries were sitting together talking
about the day's events, they heard a piercing wail, which went
on and on, coming from the direction of the nearby village.
They afterwards found out that one of the warriors who had
been injured in the fighting had since died from his wounds.
The villagers had then killed the dead man's widow and both
the bodies were taken out to sea to be buried. It was the custom
to kill a wife when her husband died. They believed that by this
means the wife's spirit would accompany her husband to the
next world, where she would continue to serve him as she had
done on earth.

John and the other missionaries knew that the natives
would never abandon their cruel ways until they came to know
for themselves the love of God and received salvation from
their sins through faith in the Lord Jesus Christ. They were
therefore very keen to learn the islanders' language as quickly
as possible so that they could begin to teach these people about
the one true God and the way of salvation.

Groups of islanders would often gather to watch as John
and the other missionaries built their homes, chattering and
laughing among themselves and pointing at things which
caught their eye. One day one of the men picked up something
belonging to the missionaries and asked his friend, 'Nungsi
nari enu?' John guessed he was asking, 'What is this?' So,
picking up a piece of wood, he looked at the men and said,

'Nungsi nari enu?' The men looked at each other as if to say, 'He can speak our language now,' and then told him the word for wood in their language. Once John had learnt that phrase, he was soon able to discover the names of various other everyday objects.

Another day, a stranger pointed at John and asked, 'Se nangin?' John guessed that the man was asking his name, so he pointed at the man and asked the same question.

Once he had learnt those two phrases John and his companions were soon able to find out the names of most of the people and the objects which they saw around them. John would write down every new word he learnt, spelling it according to the way it was pronounced, as the language spoken by the islanders had never before been written down and did not even have its own alphabet. However, the islanders did not always tell John the right words, and sometimes he misunderstood what they said, so his learning of the language did not proceed as quickly as he would have liked, especially at first. But in time, as he began to get a grasp of the language, and as the natives became more used to him and more interested in helping him, he made better progress.

John and Mary were anxious to move into their new house before the rainy season, so, even though the house was not yet finished, John went back to Aneityum to collect Mary and bring her to the island. They found a trading ship which was willing to transport them, with all their boxes, and on 5 November 1858 they landed on Tanna to begin their life on the island together. Later, John was to bitterly regret bringing Mary to the island at the start of the rainy season, when the risk of catching a fever was greatest, but no one had told them of the dangers and she did not want to be left behind in Aneityum without her husband.

Mary was delighted with her new home and wrote to her parents, 'I have never seen such a lovely spot.' Within a few weeks she had made friends with some of the local women and begun to teach some of the little girls singing and sewing. She was expecting their first child and, as John put the finishing touches to their new home, they were both really looking forward to their new life there.

But, sadly, it was not to last. In February 1859, only three months after their arrival on Tanna, Mary became ill with a fever. For a day or two after the birth of their baby son Peter on 12 February, she seemed to improve, and they were both full of joy and thanksgiving to the Lord. However, within a short time the fever returned and Mary became very ill again. Eventually, on 3 March 1859, she passed away to be with her Lord and Saviour.

Just before she died she told Joseph Copeland, who had come in to see her, 'You must not think that I regret coming here... If I had the same thing to do over again, I would do it with far more pleasure, yes, with all my heart. Oh, no! I do not regret leaving home and friends, though at the time I felt it keenly.'

John was griefstricken at her death, though he told himself over and over again that she was 'not lost, only gone before to be for ever with the Lord'. To add to his grief, only a couple of weeks later his baby son Peter also became ill and died.

We can only try to imagine how John must have felt at that time. He was weak and ill from fever and said afterwards that if it had not been for the grace of the Lord, which sustained him in this great trial, and for the sense of fellowship with the Lord Jesus that never completely deserted him, 'I must have gone mad and died beside that lonely grave.' He missed his wife terribly and, while he did not claim to understand the reason why God had allowed Mary and baby Peter to die, he believed with all his heart that his God only did what was right. He was absolutely certain that, in his own words, 'My God and Father was too wise and loving to err in anything that he does or permits.' So he 'looked up to the Lord for help, and struggled on in his work'.

The grave was to become a very sacred place where he would often go
to weep and pray

John dug the grave for Mary and the baby with his own hands and carefully decorated it with pieces of white coral. That grave was to become a very sacred place to him, where he would often go in the years ahead to weep and pray in faith and hope that one day God would send his Holy Spirit into the hearts of the natives of Tanna, causing them to turn in faith to Jesus Christ as their Lord and Saviour.

To think about

Only a little while before this book was published a monument was erected on the island of Tanna in memory of Mary Paton and her son Peter. As we travel about we find monuments to great Christians.

It is important to remember the saints who gave a lifetime of service to Christ and in some cases were murdered bearing witness to the Christ they loved. As we read the Bible we are encouraged to walk in their footsteps. Unless monuments are erected to the memory of great Christians and books written about their exploits for Christ we lose a great part of our history.

Try to get hold of some books about great Christians and as you read you will be encouraged to serve Christ faithfully. Make a list of great missionaries of the last two or three centuries. I think you will be surprised at how few you know.

Build up your library and read. Then encourage other members of your family and friends to read widely too. Great blessings might come your way through such an endeavour.

8.
Threats of death

John was soon to discover that the men and women of Tanna were a very religious people in their own, misguided way. They believed in many gods and worshipped the spirits of their heroes and ancestors, using idols made from wood or stone, as well as relics made from pieces of the dead person's hair or fingernails. They lived in constant fear of these idols, and treated them with great respect. Whenever any tragedy or disaster occurred on the island they put it down to one of the evil spirits in which they believed. Their whole religion consisted of trying to ward off troubles by placating the angry spirits. As far as John could tell, they had no idea that there could be a God of love and mercy, but only evil powers who were to be feared. Nor did they have any sense of sin against God and his laws, or of the need for forgiveness.

These people did have some dim idea of a heaven which they called Aneai. This was also the name of one of their villages, which was situated on the highest and most beautiful spot on the island. When they tried to imagine the promised land of their dreams they thought of it in terms of the most beautiful place that they had ever seen, which was this village.

When the missionaries began to speak to them about the true God and the way to heaven through faith in the Lord Jesus Christ, at first they were interested. However, when they were told they would have to give up all their false gods and their evil ways, they became angry with the missionaries and began to cause trouble for them.

Each village had at least one sacred man. The other villagers presented him with gifts in the hope that he would be able to win the favour of the unseen spirits who they believed to be in control of everything — life and death, the weather, health and sickness, war and peace. These sacred men claimed that they could put a curse on a person or a tribe. They would do this by pronouncing a spell over some object, such as the skin of a banana, which had been touched by the person to be cursed. The sacred men also claimed to be able to remove any sickness or hurt caused by the evil spirit.

When things went wrong, or the spells cast by the sacred men would not work, they would blame the missionaries and their 'new religion'. Whenever they did so, John and his companions faced great danger from the tribespeople.

On one occasion an old and well-respected chief from Aneityum, named Nowhat, visited Tanna. Soon after returning home he became ill and died. The Tannese people decided John Paton and his new form of worshp were to blame for the old man's death. They talked of burning down John's house and killing all the missionaries, or at least forcing them to leave the island. Nowhat's brother came over to Tanna to try to convince the Tannese that the missionaries were not to blame, but he was not able to hold proper talks with them because he could not speak their language and there was no one to interpret for him. Two days after he landed, he too became very ill. That only made things worse! Now the natives were sure that it was the missionaries and their friends who brought sickness and death!

The tribesmen held meetings at which their leaders gave rousing speeches, inciting hatred against the missionaries. They even held feasts at which they ate the bodies of women they had killed in sacrifice to their gods. John and the other missionaries were powerless to do anything to save the women and they knew that at any moment it might be their turn to be killed and eaten!

But God was not going to let the missionaries be killed! First, two of the local chiefs took the side of the missionaries and for a time they were able to stop the others from attacking or killing John and his companions.

Then a meeting of the chiefs was called and the majority decided to choose a band of men to kill all the missionaries and anyone else who stood up for them. Suddenly, in the midst of the excitement and blood-curdling war-cries, one of the great warrior chiefs leapt to his feet, swinging his huge club in the air and bringing it crashing to earth. When he had the attention of everyone present he warned them all in a very loud voice: 'The man that kills Missi must first kill me — the men that kill the mission teachers must first kill me and my people — for we shall stand by them and defend them till death!'

No sooner had he spoken than another chief stood up and announced that he too would defend the missionaries. The meeting then broke up in confusion and the lives of the missionaries and their helpers were saved.

John and his companions thanked God with all their hearts for saving them, as it were, out of the very jaws of the lions. They knew it was God who had intervened, putting it into the hearts of the two chiefs to stand up for them. John remembered that he had once treated the wounds of a brother of one of these chiefs after a fight. Perhaps it was this small act of kindness which God had used to make the chief speak up for him and so to save his life as well as the lives of the other Christians.

On another occasion there was a drought and the bananas and other crops started to wither. Once again the natives blamed the missionaries and their God. After a meeting of all the island chiefs, the great chief Nouka and his nephew Miaki,

the war-chief, came to see John in great alarm. They told him
that two of the powerful chiefs who lived inland had threatened to kill them and their people, as well as all the Christians,
if they did not kill the missionaries or drive them out of the
island — unless the rain came first, and plenty of it! They
begged John and the others: 'Pray to your Jehovah God for
rain, and do not go far beyond your door for a time; we are all
in greatest danger, and if war breaks out, we fear we cannot
protect you.'

The following Lord's Day, as the Christians gathered for
worship, it began to rain heavily. The islanders believed that
the Christians' God had sent the rain in answer to their prayers,
so for a time they were permitted to stay on. However, as the
heavy rain continued, the damp weather brought the usual
fevers and other illnesses. Then the weather turned stormy and
the violent winds damaged the fruit trees. So once again the
superstitious islanders blamed the Christians and their God for
sending these sicknesses and troubles.

Sometimes, too, the missionaries were blamed for the
troubles caused by other white men who came to the islands to
trade, many of whom were very cruel to the islanders. To the
natives all white men were the same and when they suffered at
the hands of the traders they were likely to take revenge on the
Christians, simply because they too were white, even though
they had only shown kindness to the people. It was also the
traders who supplied the islanders with guns and other weapons, in exchange for sandalwood or other local produce. The
sale of weapons only encouraged the natives to keep fighting
and killing each other.

On one occasion the tribesmen on the nearby island of
Erromanga murdered three of the traders and the natives who
worked for them in revenge for the dreadful treatment they had
received at the hands of white men. When the local chiefs on
Tanna heard of this, they all sat around over their evening

Sketch of Erromanga by Margaret Paton

meal, talking about the news and getting very drunk. That night, while they were all sleeping off the effects of the drink, a group of tribesmen from another part of the island crept up on them in the dark and fired a shot, killing one man. This was the signal for war between the two tribes.

Early next morning, Miaki, the war-chief, had a herald sound a call to battle on the conch shell. The noise could be heard six miles away! A great fight followed, with armed men rushing back and forth waving clubs, spears and tomahawks and every now and then firing off a musket. After the local men had driven off the invaders and then been chased in their turn, both sides sat down, glaring and shouting insults at each other.

Eventually, tempers cooled and chiefs from both sides came to John's house to ask him to tend their wounded men. He did so, and at the same time begged them to stop fighting each other. He extracted a promise from them, but it was soon forgotten, for only a few weeks later, when John returned to the island after spending a fortnight on Aneityum to recover from an illness, he discovered that eight of the local people had been killed in another attack. So it was that the inhabitants of Tanna lived with the threat of war hanging over their heads from day to day.

All the young boys were trained to fight from a very early age. They were taught how to shoot accurately with a bow and arrows and to throw a spear at a target until they could hit it every time. They learned how to a wield a club or a tomahawk and, when guns were available, to shoot with a musket or revolver. The adult men would spend all their time when they were not fighting in relaxing and feasting, while all the hard work was done by the women and girls. It was the women who grew all the crops, cut and prepared the stakes used for fencing and carried all the heavy burdens.

It was a very hard life on Tanna for girls and women. They were just slaves of the men, who were very cruel to them, often

A Tannese family about 1850

beating them for the slightest little thing and sometimes even killing them as sacrifices to the gods, after which the bodies were cooked and eaten. When one of the chiefs became seriously ill, the sacred men sacrificed three women in the hope that this would satisfy the spirits and bring about his recovery.

On one occasion when John tried to stop a man from beating his wife outside the mission house, the man came back with a group of his friends, all of them carrying weapons, and threatened to kill the missionaries for interfering. However, John bravely stood his ground and, trusting the Lord to watch over him, told the man, in front of all the armed warriors, that he was a bad man and a coward because of the way he treated his wife. After some very tense moments, the man at last lowered his club to the ground and said that he was sorry and would mend his ways.

When John tried to persuade some of the chiefs to put a stop to the cruelty to women and children one of the chiefs actually told him, 'If we did not beat our women they would never work; they would not fear and obey us; but when we have beaten and killed, and feasted on two or three, the rest are all very quiet and good for a long time!'

John tried to show them that if they were kind to their wives, instead of beating them, the women would actually work better and everyone would be happier, but the chiefs claimed that their women 'could not understand kindness'. Eventually a few of the chiefs agreed not to allow any more beating of wives or killing of widows when their husbands died.

However, John found that the most effective way of getting the men to change their ways was to show them by example how Christians should behave. So whenever he needed any wood for the house, he would get several of his helpers to come along with him accompanied by their wives. (These helpers were Christians from Aneityum who had come over with their families to help the missionaries teach the people.) When they had finished cutting the wood, each of the men would pick up a large bundle to carry, while John gave each of the women only a very small bundle. On the way back, whenever they met any of the local men John would explain that this was the way that Christians treated their wives and sisters. He said that this was why Christian families were happy ones, with all the members loving one another and all taking a share in the work, each doing the jobs for which they were best fitted.

The chiefs also agreed to tell their people not to do their ordinary work on the Lord's Day. After he had been on Tanna for about a year, John began holding public worship services each Sunday. About ten of the chiefs used to attend, bringing their wives and families. After the service was over John and his companions would visit as many of the local villages as they could, speaking to the people about the Lord Jesus. Sometimes they would make a circuit of several villages, which meant walking ten or twelve miles each way. When they could get enough people to sit around and listen they would hold a simple service of worship to the one true God. It was very hard work and at times John felt discouraged at the lack of interest shown by the people. However, these visits helped the missionaries to get to know the people and to learn their language, both of which were important if they were to be able to teach them more about the Lord.

In time some of the men began to visit John at night, when no one else could see them (like Nicodemus who came to see the Lord Jesus in the dark). If John shut all the doors and drew all the blinds they would stay for hours asking him questions about his 'new religion' and learning from him the teaching of the Bible. One of his visitors told John, 'I would be an Awfuaki man [that is, a Christian] were it not that all the rest would laugh at me; that I could not stand.'

After a while the wife of one of these men died. The chief came to John and said he wanted to wrap his wife's body in a calico sheet and bury her in a proper grave, just as he had seen John bury his wife Mary. When John offered to attend the funeral and pray at the graveside, the chief said 'No', because if John came many of the villagers would stay away. He said that the old chief Nowar had promised to take the service for him and pray to Jehovah, the God of the Christians. This was the first funeral service ever held among the Tannese people and it caused a lot of interest.

Afterwards people began asking John questions. They were particularly interested in what he had to say about the resurrection from the dead. John and his friends seized every possible opportunity to tell them about the life and death of the Lord Jesus, who had come to save men and women like them, making them fit to go to heaven, where they would live with him for ever.

To think about

It is easy to imagine what an idol on Tanna was like. However, people today have their idols too. Make a list of idols that occupy the minds of men and women today.

In your reading you will have noticed that the natives did all they could to win favour with their tribal gods — even resorting to human sacrifice. Today some Christians believe they can do something to win God's favour.

You probably know Christian people who have the idea that if they pray a little longer, read a few extra words of Scripture, put more money on the plate and do a few good turns, God will be especially nice to them — that God will then owe them something. Are they right? Does God ever owe us anything? Why does God bless his people in so many ways?

9.
You shall not steal — or kill

Another problem from which John regularly suffered was the theft of his possessions. If he caught any of the natives in the act of stealing something and tried to stop them, they would threaten him with a club or a tomahawk. But usually he did not actually see the theft, because they were very skilful at taking things without getting caught. If one of them saw a small object lying on the floor of John's home, such as a knife or a pair of scissors, he would edge towards it until he could cover it with his foot, all the time looking John in the face as he did so. Then the man would wrap his toes round the article and calmly walk away with it still hidden under one foot. Other things would be quickly snatched up when John was not looking and hidden away among the thick layer of tiny woven plaits which covered their heads, or under a hairy armpit.

They had no sense of shame about stealing, but only about being caught in the act. No one would ever admit to knowing anything about stolen property. They thought it clever to tell lies, in which they protested their innocence.

One day John had hung his bed-clothes out on a line to dry. To make sure they did not disappear he stood with the wives of two of his Christian helpers keeping an eye on the line of washing.

Suddenly the war-chief Miaki came rushing up. 'Missi,' he called urgently, 'come in, quick, quick! I want to tell you something and to get your advice!' As he spoke he led the way into the house and John was obliged to follow him. A few moments later John heard shouts coming from the two women he had left outside guarding his drying bed-clothes: 'Missi, Missi, come quick! Miaki's men are stealing your sheets and blankets.'

By the time John ran outside again, all the sheets and blankets had disappeared and there was no sign of the thieves. Of course, Miaki denied that he had deliberately distracted John to allow his men to steal the bed-clothes. He pretended to be very angry with the thieves, beating the bushes with his club and shouting, 'Thus will I smash these fellows, and compel them to return your clothes.' However, the stolen property was not returned and when John later challenged Miaki about his promise the chief just made excuses. It was obvious that he had never really intended to do anything about the theft. In fact he had probably taken his share of the stolen goods.

The islanders stole almost everything John owned. His fowls, goats and cooking utensils — even his kettle — all disappeared. When John appealed for the return of his property the chief pretended to be furious with the thieves, but no thief was ever found and nothing was returned. At last, in desperation, John offered a blanket as a reward to the person who brought back his kettle. Eventually Miaki himself brought it back, claiming to have had great difficulty in finding it. So John could now boil water for a cup of tea. But the lid of the kettle was still missing.

There was nothing that John could do except to take all his problems to the Lord in prayer and trust in the God of all grace to support him through the difficult time. He was convinced that if only the Tannese people came to love and serve the Lord

Jesus they would soon learn to treat the missionaries as their helpers and friends, instead of trying to cheat and harm them at every turn, but in the meantime the going was hard, especially as he was now the only European missionary on that part of the island, since his friend Joseph Copeland had gone to one of the other mission stations to help there.

Then one morning a number of the islanders came running to John's house in a state of great excitement. 'Missi, Missi,' they were shouting, 'there is a god or a ship on fire, or something of fear, coming over the sea! We see no flames, but it smokes like a volcano. Is it a spirit, a god, or a ship on fire? What is it? What is it?'

John thought quickly and saw an opportunity of getting some of his stolen property back.

'I cannot go at once,' he replied. 'I must first dress in my best clothes; it will likely be one of Queen Victoria's men-of-war, coming to ask me if your conduct is good or bad, if you are stealing my property, or threatening my life, or how you are using me.'

Soon afterwards, the two frightened chiefs came running up to ask, 'Missi, will it be a ship of war?'

John still refused to go and look, but replied, 'I think it will.'

By now the chiefs were really worried. 'Missi,' they asked, 'only tell us, will he ask you if we have been stealing your things?'

John replied, 'I expect he will.'

'And will you tell him?' the chiefs wanted to know.

'I must tell him the truth. If he asks, I will tell him,' was John' answer.

'Oh, Missi, don't tell him!' pleaded the two chiefs. 'Everything shall be brought back to you at once, and no one will be allowed again to steal from you.'

'Be quick!' John told them. 'Everything must be returned before he comes.'

By now, John was enjoying the situation. He could not help being amused because up till that point in time no one had ever admitted knowing anything about the stolen property, or being able to do anything to get it back. Now people came running from all sides carrying pots, pans, blankets and other objects which had been stolen from his house. Soon there was a large pile of the stolen goods outside his door.

The chiefs came hurrying back, out of breath from all their rushing about, and asked, 'Missi, Missi, do tell us, is the stolen property all here?'

John really had no idea and obviously there was no time to check, but he ran outside, took a quick look at the pile and said, 'I don't see the lid of the kettle there yet!'

'No,' admitted one of the chiefs, 'for it is on the other side of the island.' He begged John not to tell the ship's captain it was missing because he had sent for it, 'and it will be here tomorrow'!

John then insisted that the three chiefs, Nauka, Miaki and Nowar, should wait with him to greet the captain, saying that if they ran away the great man would want to know why they were afraid. John would then have to tell him about all the thefts and the threats against his life. The chiefs were frightened at the thought of meeting Queen Victoria's representative, so they promised that there would be no more trouble.

As they all stood watching, H.M.S. *Cordelia* steamed into the harbour. The captain had heard reports of the dangers faced by John and the other missionaries and had come to see if he could help in any way.

Captain Vernon came ashore dressed in full naval uniform, which made a great impression upon the assembled chiefs and islanders. Miaki, the war-chief, rushed off and dressed himself in an old coat which had once belonged to a soldier, evidently hoping to impress the captain, but only succeeded in making himself look ridiculous.

The visit of Captain Vernon from H.M.S. *Cordelia*

With his courage returning, Chief Miaki made a request: 'Missi, this great chief, whom Queen Victoria has sent to visit you in her man-of-war, cannot go over the whole island so as to be seen by all our people; and I wish to ask you to ask him if he will stand by a tree, and allow me to put a spear on the ground at his heel, and we will make a nick in it at the top of his head, and the spear will be sent round the island to let all the people see how tall this great man is!' Captain Vernon was only too glad to oblige and that spear was to become a talking-point all round the island for many days to come.

Captain Vernon wanted to do what he could to help protect the missionaries from attack. He decided to show the natives something of the awesome fighting power of his ship. He felt sure that a demonstration of the guns firing would terrify the natives and might deter them from harming the missionaries if they thought that a visit from a man-of-war would be the result of any action against the white men.

So he issued an invitation to the chiefs to meet him the next day. At the agreed time twenty warrior chiefs turned up at the mission house, all carrying their weapons. After sitting with them for a time and warning them against doing any harm to visitors to the island (which, of course, included the mission-aries), Captain Vernon invited them to accompany him on board his ship. The warriors were very impressed by the sight of all the ship's weapons, especially the big guns. When the sailors fired a couple of shots out to sea, causing a big splash, the islanders began to grow nervous. Then a shot was fired in the direction of the island itself. The cannon-ball ripped its way through a coconut grove, tearing trees to pieces as if they were just pieces of straw. The chiefs were terrified and could not wait to be safely back on dry ground! For many years to come they would tell stories about the day when the great 'fire god of the sea and the Captain of the great white Queen' visited their island!

The H.M.S. *Cordelia* was not the only notable ship to call at Tanna. Some time later the *Camden Packet*, a whaling ship loaded with a valuable cargo of sperm oil, commanded by a Captain Allen, called at Tanna. The captain was a Christian and John was invited to conduct worship on board. The ship's carpenter repaired John's mission-boat, which had been damaged on a reef, and refused to accept any payment for helping a fellow Christian. After purchasing fruit, coconuts and other foodstuffs from the local people the ship sailed out of the harbour. On this occasion, because the captain was an honest man, the islanders were fairly treated and paid in full for the goods purchased. Sadly, this was often not the case when trading-ships called at the island.

Another time a large ship, all fitted up and armed like a man-of-war, arrived in the harbour. It belonged to a Frenchman and was manned by slaves, whom the captain treated very harshly. However, he was kind to John and, learning of the dangers he faced on Tanna, offered to take him to Sydney, or any other place of safety he might wish to name. But John knew that God had a work for him to carry out on the island and was afraid that if he left, even for a short trip, he would not be allowed to return, so he thanked the captain but declined his offer.

By this time John had decided to move his house to higher ground. After the death of his wife and baby son, he had himself been ill on many occasions with malarial fever. On one occasion the illness left him so weak that Abraham, an old Christian teacher from Aneityum, and his wife Nafatu had to help him to crawl up to higher ground. When he could go no further the kindly couple carried him the rest of the way. After several days in the cooler breezes on the hilltop, where he was cared for by Abraham and his wife, John began to recover. Then, with their help, he set about the construction of his new house on the hilltop, using planks from an old ship which he had bought from one of the traders who called at the island. In time he hoped also to construct a church-building beside the house. He made a point of paying, in full view of everyone, all of the islanders who had a claim to any part of this hilltop area, so that there could be no disputes afterwards concerning his right to the land.

John thought that while the Frenchman's ship was still in the harbour it would be a good time to take down his old house by the shore (which the islanders had threatened to burn down) and use the wood to enlarge his new home on the hilltop. To do this he and his helpers removed the thatched roof of the old house and set it alight. Unfortunately he had not thought to tell the French captain of his plans.

Seeing the smoke and flames and believing the worst, the captain ordered his men to load the ship's guns, while he rushed ashore with a large party of armed men. In broken English he exclaimed, 'Where are they? 'Where are they? The scoundrels! I will do for them and protect you. I shall punish them, the scoundrels!' He was so excited that John had trouble convincing him it was all right and he was only burning the thatch which he no longer needed. When the captain finally understood, he burst out laughing. All the same, before he left, he took the opportunity to call the local chiefs together and warn them that if any harm were to befall John he would come back with his ship to kill them and set fire to their villages.

Not all the ships which visited the island were so welcome. Many of them belonged to unscrupulous traders who did not care how badly they treated the islanders or what would be the consequences of selling guns to them. These men were only concerned in making money from such sales. Some of them were to cause a lot of trouble for John and the other missonaries.

One of these traders, a Captain Winchester, decided to set up home on Tanna with a native wife. He bartered with the islanders for their pigs and poultry, which he then sold to passing ships. In return he sold the natives guns and ammunition. His trade depended upon war, so he was continually stirring up the chiefs to keep fighting one another.

Miaki, the war-chief, had a younger brother called Rarip, who was about eighteen years old. When fighting broke out, encouraged by this trader, Rarip came to live with John because he wanted no part in it. After a time Miaki forced Rarip to join the warriors, but he ran away and returned to John saying, 'Missi, I hate this fighting; it is not good to kill men; I will live with you!'

However, before long Miaki came looking for his brother. Finding him with John, he forced Rarip to go back with him to battle, where he was shot and killed in the opening skirmish.

As soon as he heard the news, John hurried to the village where preparations were being made for the burial of young Rarip. He saw the women and girls tearing their hair in their grief, uttering loud wails and cutting themselves with sharp pieces of bamboo and even broken glass. The men too were cutting themselves with knives and howling in distress. John was deeply distressed at the sight. He said afterwards, describing the scene at the funeral, 'My heart broke to see them and to think that they knew not to look to our dear Lord Jesus for consolation.'

John then offered to fetch a white sheet, in which to wrap the body of the dead Rarip. He also offered to conduct a Christian burial. The natives recognized this action as a mark of respect for the dead man, so they readily agreed. At the graveside John read the Scriptures, prayed and sang a psalm of praise to God. All the time he was filled with a deep longing for the day when these people would really come to believe the gospel and so share the Christian hope of a wonderful life beyond death, in the presence of Christ and all God's people.

As the war continued many other warriors were killed. Chief Miaki then turned against Captain Winchester, who had sold them the weapons and encouraged them to fight. He threatened to kill the trader in revenge for the death of his brother and the other warriors. When the captain begged John to let him and his wife sleep at the mission house for safety, John said, 'No!' Under no circumstances did he want to be associated in the minds of the tribespeople with the man and his evil ways. The trader was so afraid that he slept each night in a small boat anchored right out in the middle of the bay, well away from the shore. Finally, to the relief of everyone, he and his wife fled the island when a trading ship called in. However, the war he had started still dragged on.

Each Lord's Day during that unhappy time, John held services which were attended by many of the islanders. At first these services were only for the local tribespeople who lived by the shore. When John spoke of going to speak and pray with those on the other side in the fighting, they told him, 'Missi, pray only for us, and your God will be strong to help us…! You must not pray with the enemy, lest he may help them too.' After that he made a point of visiting both camps and holding worship services with men from both sides, at which he told them that his God was angry with all war and would not fight for either. John then begged the warring tribes to live in peace with each other as God had commanded.

To think about

John faced a really hostile, devious people on the island of Tanna and there can be no doubt that the display of force by the British battleship helped to save his life and the life of others who lived and worked in that area.

In our society many are opposed to the use of force and threats to achieve any ends — even the good behaviour of men and women, or children.

In the Scriptures Christ is more often recorded as speaking about hell than about heaven. In Proverbs the use of the 'rod' is encouraged in certain situations. We also read of God chastening his people to make them more holy.

A thought of hell for those who do not repent of their sins is often the means used by God to turn people to Christ for salvation. Do you know your eternal destiny? What is the way of salvation?

10.
Dangers all around

The Tannese warriors lived for their wars and any promises they made to John that they would keep the peace meant very little. At one time twenty chiefs promised to live in peace with each other, but within a very short time several warriors were murdered and war loomed again.

On one occasion John set out with Abraham and another of the Christian teachers in an effort to meet some of the hostile tribesmen who lived further inland. They hoped that, by talking to them, they might be able to avert another war. After walking through the bush for some time, the three men suddenly came upon the natives in the middle of a feast on the village common. When they saw John and the others approaching the men leapt to their feet, brandishing their weapons.

John and his companions, who were, of course, all unarmed, walked steadily forward into the centre of the group. At the same time John tried to make himself heard above all the noise. 'My love to you all, men of Tanna!' he called out. 'Fear not; I am your friend. I love you every one, and am come to tell you about Jehovah God and good conduct such as pleases him.'

One of the chiefs then came up to John, took him by the hand, and invited him to sit down and talk. While a few ran off in fright, many of the warriors began dancing in a circle round the newcomers, beating time with their clubs on an upturned canoe. 'Missi is come! Missi is come!' they shouted out in great excitement. The men and boys gathered round, while the women and younger children peeped out of the bushes when they thought no one was looking.

After an hour or so, during which a lot of questions were asked, John was allowed to conduct a short worship service. Then the village leaders shook hands with the Christians, promising that they would not harm anyone connected with the mission. The villagers gave John presents of coconuts, pieces of sugar cane and two fowls. In return John gave the supreme chief a bright red shirt, and handed out fish-hooks and lengths of calico to be shared among the rest.

When John and his companions returned home, laden with gifts, the local people could scarcely believe their eyes. Such a thing had never happened on the island before. When they had heard where John and his friends had gone they had been sure that they would not return, because the inland tribes would have killed and eaten them! That time the peace lasted a little over four weeks. That was a long time by the standards of the island!

Early one morning John found his house surrounded by armed warriors and was told that they had come to kill him. He knelt down to pray, thinking this might well be the last prayer he uttered on earth. Then he went out to face the warriors. After reminding them that he had given them no cause to treat him unkindly, he warned them of what probably would happen to them if they killed him.

After a while, one of them stood up and said, 'Our conduct has been bad; but now we will fight for you, and kill all those who hate you.' At that, John grabbed hold of the leader and would not let him go until he promised not to kill anyone on his behalf. He explained that the Lord had taught his followers to love their enemies and to return good for evil.

Although that meeting broke up with promises of friendship and protection, soon afterwards a gathering of all the
chiefs decided that John should be killed as they 'hated
Jehovah and the worship'. They told John he was welcome to
stay and trade with them, if he would only give up praying and
talking about his God. They wanted to carry on with their old
way of life.

John explained that the only reason he had come to the
island was to teach them about the one true God and to lead
them to know and serve this God for themselves.

One chief then spoke out on behalf of all present: 'Missi,
our fathers loved and worshipped whom you call the devil, the
Evil Spirit; and we are determined to do the same, for we love
the conduct of our fathers.' The chief went on to talk about the
earlier missionaries, who had tried to change their form of
worship, but whom they had driven out or killed. 'After each
of these acts,' he said, 'Tanna was good; we all lived like our
fathers, and sickness and death left us. Now, our people are
determined to kill you, if you do not leave this island; for you
are changing our customs and destroying our worship, and we
hate the Jehovah worship.'

This man had travelled to Australia and knew something of
life outside the island. He complained that 'The people of
Sydney belong to your Britain; they know what is right and
wrong as well as you; and we have ourselves seen them
fishing, feasting, cooking, working, and seeking pleasure on
the Sabbath as on any other day... We have seen the people do
all the conduct at Sydney which you call bad, but which we
love. You are but one, they are many; they are right, and you
must be wrong; you are teaching lies for worship.'

A lot more arguing and discussing followed, but eventually
John was able to explain some of the benefits which a knowledge of the true God brought to people of other lands. He was
even allowed to conduct a short time of worship before
leaving.

But only a few days later a crowd of armed men gathered outside John's house and one of them suddenly rushed at John with his axe raised. In the nick of time one of the chiefs standing nearby grabbed a spade which John had just been using and managed to avert the blow, thus saving the missionary's life.

The following day a chief armed with a loaded gun followed John about for hours, threatening to shoot him. All the time John quietly went about his work as if the man were not there, praying silently to the Lord for his protection as he did so.

Another time a group of armed men tried to break into his house at night, but were frightened off by his little dog. Soon afterwards there was a plot to set the house on fire and club the Christians to death as they tried to escape, but one of the teachers learnt of it in time and the plot was frustrated.

John did not find it easy, facing danger and possible death almost every day, but he knew that God had a work for him to do and would preserve him until that work was done. He carried on with his daily life and work, trusting the Lord to take care of him. In fact he found that his experiences of danger and God's deliverance from them strengthened his faith. He was never as conscious of the Lord's presence with him, protecting him and giving him the strength he needed to go on, as he was in those days when he faced the danger of death almost every hour. He found great comfort in the promise of Christ: 'Lo, I am with you always, even unto the end of the world.' He was so conscious of the Lord's power supporting him that he was able to say with Paul, 'I can do all things through Christ who strengthens me.'

It was not only John who was in danger. Namuri, one of the Aneityumese Christian teachers, had set up house with his wife in a nearby village, where he began teaching the local people about the Lord and leading in worship. One day one of the sacred men threw a stone weapon at him, trying to kill him,

A typical native Christian teacher

and then attacked him with a club. Namuri was badly injured,
but managed to escape to John's house. With loving care John
nursed him back to health, and he returned once more to his
village. When John urged him to stay at the mission house a
while longer, Namuri explained, 'Missi, when I see them
thirsting for my blood, I just see myself when the missionary
first came to my island. I desired to murder him, as they now
desire to kill me. Had he stayed away for such danger, I would
have remained heathen; but he came, and continued coming to
teach us, till, by the grace of God, I was changed to what I am.
Now the same God that changed me to this, can change these
poor Tannese to love and serve him. I cannot stay away from

them, but I will sleep at the mission house, and do all I can by day to bring them to Jesus.'

For a few weeks all went well, but then one morning during the worship service the same sacred man who had attacked him earlier crept up on Namuri while he was praying and attacked him with his club, leaving him to die. Namuri managed to crawl back to the mission house, where John again tended him, but sadly was unable to save his life.

Namuri was in a lot of pain from his wounds, but he was able to rejoice that soon he would be with his Lord Jesus. He kept repeating the words, 'For the sake of Jesus! For Jesu's sake!' and praying for the people who had injured him: 'O Lord Jesus, forgive them, for they do not know what they are doing. Oh, do not take away all your servants from Tanna! Do not take away your worship from this dark island! O God, bring all the Tannese to love and follow Jesus!' And so, echoing the words of Stephen, the first martyr, he went to be with the Lord he loved.

John prepared a coffin for Namuri's body and buried him near the mission house. The Christians wept at the loss of their friend, but knew that one day they would meet him again in glory. It was the joy of seeing people like Namuri, who had once hated the Christians, coming to know and love the Lord that made the hardships of missionary work all worthwhile for John and the other missionaries on those islands.

Sometimes danger came in other forms, too. Some of the fish which were caught in the waters round Tanna were highly poisonous. A native woman made friends with the wife of one of the Christian teachers and started bringing her gifts of food. But her friendship was not what it seemed. She prepared a meal using a fish which was known to be poisonous and took it to the teacher's wife as a gift. She then boasted to a friend of what she had done. Hearing this, a friendly neighbour tried to warn the teacher's wife not to eat the meal, but it was too late.

There was no known antidote to the poison and the poor woman died in agony. Like Namuri, she too was a true Christian who had willingly risked her life to serve the Lord. Again the missionaries found comfort in the knowledge that she had gone to be with the Lord whom she loved.

Nor was it only the islanders who caused trouble for John and his companions. The captain of one of the ships engaged in the sandalwood trade tried to cheat John out of a boat which had been sent over to him from the mission. The man lied, saying that Joseph Copeland had authorized him to take it. When John tried to stop him taking the boat, the man not only swore at him, but began knocking him about and kicking him. This incident only made things even more difficult for John, for the islanders then said among themselves, 'When a white man from his own country can so pull and knock the mission-ary about, and steal his boat and chain without being punished for it, we also may do as we please!'

It was largely because of the way the sandalwood traders treated the islanders that they had come to mistrust and hate all white men, including the missionaries. Indeed they often had good reason to wish that white men had never set foot on their island. The traders not only robbed the natives, stealing everything they could find of any value, even the children's food, but were ready to murder anyone who tried to stop them. Some of them even lured men and women on board their ships and carried them off to work in other parts of the world as slaves. They looked down on the natives and were quite prepared to see them all die and have their lands taken over by white men. It was hardly surprising, then, that the islanders who had suffered at the hands of these men were ready to take revenge on all white men and thought nothing of stealing from them and killing them.

One of the traders, who had stored his goods in a cellar under his house, used to sleep over the trapdoor which was the only entrance into this cellar. The area all round his house was patrolled by armed men and savage guard dogs. This man had treated some of the islanders very badly, so they got together and successfully dug a tunnel underground, burrowing their way into the cellar. Then they rolled the barrels of tobacco, ammunition and other goods through the tunnel while the trader and his guards thought they were all safely locked away!

John had himself been the victim of theft and would have been the first to speak out against acts of revenge, but he would not have been human if he had not felt some amusement when he learnt how the islanders had got the better of that cruel trader. He may even have thought that the man had got just what he deserved!

To think about

John Paton was a brave man who showed no fear of death. As we read the Scriptures we discover that the saints also had no fear of dying. The apostle Paul was able to write, 'For me to live is Christ, and to die is gain' (Philippians 1:21). We need to know that death is the doorway to the presence of Christ and all who love Christ should be able to say with Paul that they have 'a desire to depart and to be with Christ, which is far better' than anything the world has to offer (Philippians 1:23).

Today there are many people who are afraid of death and will not even talk about dying. If you knew you were going to die very soon, would you be ready to face God? How do you know?

We all need to read and digest the wonderful things God has to say about heaven and the glory that awaits all who are saved by Christ. When those truths sink into our hearts we will have a true longing to be with Christ.

11.
The sacred men meet their match

Not all the islanders were hostile to John and one of the local chiefs, Nowar, had by this time become a friend whom John felt he could trust. On more than one occasion Nowar had taken John's side and protected him when other chiefs wanted to kill him. He was one of a group of nine or ten who attended the services at the mission fairly regularly and even held a simple form of Christian worship in their own families.

Old Chief Nowar

Nowar encouraged the people from all the villages situated within nine or ten miles of the harbour to hold a great feast in honour of the Christian God, Jehovah. When they were all assembled, a party of chiefs came to escort John and the Christian teachers from Aneityum to the feast. Fourteen chiefs made speeches, one after the other, and there was a lot of talk about outlawing war on Tanna and all the tribes living in peace with one another. They agreed that there should be no more killings by witchcraft and the sacred men should stop pretending to have power over death and life or to be able to control the weather. John thought that these men probably meant what they said at the time, but he did not expect them to be able to carry it out. The Tannese people were very good at talking and making speeches, but most of what they said really meant very little and their promises came to nothing.

Following the speeches about a hundred of the men assembled in the open space in front of the crowd and went through a kind of ritual dance in which they each in turn went down on one knee, stretched out their right hands and bowed low to the ground. Then as they stood up again they began to make a howling noise which ended up as a hideous yell. Finally, they all shook hands with each other and began distributing the food. There was a large pile of food for each tribe — mainly pigs and fowls — and one meant for John and his helpers.

The two chiefs Nowar and Nerwangi then turned to John and his friends and said, 'This feast is held to move all the chiefs and people here to give up fighting, to become friends, and to worship your Jehovah God. We wish you to remain, and to teach us all good conduct. As an evidence of our sincerity, and of our love, we have prepared this pile of food for you.'

John replied by telling them how pleased he was to hear that they wanted to serve the true God and to give up fighting. He encouraged them to keep their promises, after which he presented them with gifts of calico, fish-hooks and knives. However, John could not accept their gifts of food as they had first offered the food in sacrifice to the great Evil Spirit whom they worshipped and had asked his blessing on it. John explained to them that Christians could not eat food that had been offered in sacrifice to an idol, because there was only one true God, Jehovah, and to acknowledge or serve any other God was to dishonour and displease him. John did not want to offend the tribesmen, so he made a special point of thanking them for their kind gift of the food, even though he could not eat it, and he asked the chiefs to distribute it among the people as an extra gift from the missionaries.

Then there was more pagan dancing. The men, with their faces covered in warpaint and feathers in their hair, danced in an inner circle and the women formed a larger circle round them. As they danced they sang and clapped their hands rhythmically. This was followed by a sham fight in which the women pulled blazing sticks out of the fire and pretended to attack the men with them, eventually driving them off the field. The women then danced and sang to celebrate their victory.

John could not enjoy watching the dancing and mock fighting because it was all so much associated with their pagan rituals. Describing the scene, he wrote, 'The dancing and fighting, the naked painted figures, and the constant yells and shoutings, gave one a weird sensation, and suggested strange ideas of hell broken loose.'

Finally they gathered up the food allocated to each tribe and put it all into baskets, to be taken home, since the different tribes would not sit down and eat together. Many of them stripped off their ornaments and their skirts or aprons, which were woven from grass and leaves, and gave them away to members of other tribes as gifts. They also exchanged gifts of bows and arrows and the clothes made from calico which they had received from the missionaries. The members of the various tribes all parted on the best of terms, but once the feast was over they soon went back to fighting and killing each other.

When John first built his home on Tanna the only supply of drinking water was a bubbling hot spring. In the hot climate it would often take several days for the water to cool down enough to be used. So John set about sinking a well close to the mission house. After digging down about twelve feet he found a good supply of fresh water. Soon all the local people were coming to the new well to draw water and visitors flocked from all over the island to see the amazing sight of 'rain rising up out of the earth'!

With the help of some of the natives John was also able to construct a building which he wanted to use both as a church and as a school. He bought the timber he needed for the building from the island of Aneityum and paid for it with fifty pairs of trousers and 130 yards of cloth. The trousers had been made by members of his Bible class in Glasgow, who had not forgotten their former teacher and continued to support him in his work on the missionfield.

When the church was first built people were very wary about coming to it. At the opening service there were only five men, three women and three children present in addition to John and the Christian teachers and their families.

John had brought a small printing-press to the island with him and when he had learnt enough of the Tannese language to prepare a small booklet in it, he decided to try his hand at printing. He had never done this before and found it much more difficult than building a house! He simply could not work out how to get all the pages printed in the right order. But at last, at 1 a.m. one morning, when all the islanders had been asleep for hours, he held in his hand a sheet of paper which was the first small portion of the Word of God ever to be printed in the Tannese language. John was so excited he threw his hat into the air, gave a great shout of joy and danced round the printing-press like a young boy. He realized some people might have thought his behaviour undignified, but was sure that God saw it as a true act of worship, like the time when David danced before the ark of God in his joy at seeing it finally brought to Jerusalem.

However, the superstitious islanders, who, of course, could not read for themselves, were very much afraid of books, and especially of God's book, the Bible. This was because they blamed the missionaries and their God when anything went wrong on the island, and because they were afraid that the worship of the true God would mean that they would have to change their way of life.

On one occasion when John preached to the people, encouraging them to give up their superstitious practices and to believe in and follow the true God, three of the village 'sacred men' were present. The whole population lived in fear of these three men, who claimed to have the power of life and death over them and to be able to bring sickness or health and to send rain or drought at their will. These three men now stood up and told all the people they did not believe in Jehovah, or need his help. They claimed that they could kill John by their sorcery if only they could get hold of the remains of a piece of fruit or food that he had eaten.

John decided to accept their challenge and asked God to help him show the people that really they had no power at all to harm him. He turned to a woman standing nearby, who was holding a bunch of fruit rather like plums, called quonquore, and asked if he could have some. When she told him to have as many as he wanted, he took three of the fruit, took a large bite out of each and gave the rest to the three sacred men. Then he said to all the people who were watching, 'You have seen me eat of this fruit, you have seen me give the remainder to your sacred men. They have said they can kill me by Nahak, but I challenge them to do it if they can, without arrow or spear, club or musket; for I deny that they have any power against me, or against anyone, by their sorcery.'

The village people were horrified at John's action, thinking that he would meet a horrible death, and as the sacred men began to go through the ritual of casting a spell against him many of them fled in terror, exclaiming, 'Alas Missi!' But John, who was not afraid of the sacred men, stayed to watch and from time to time teased them: 'Be quick! Stir up your gods to help you! I am not killed yet; I am perfectly well!'

Eventually, when it was obvious that nothing was going to happen to John as a result of their sorcery, the sacred men told everyone who was watching, 'We must delay till we have called all our sacred men. We will kill Missi before his next Sabbath comes round. Let all watch, for he will soon die, and that without fail.'

'Very good!' John replied. 'I challenge all your priests to unite and kill me by sorcery or Nahak. If on Sabbath next I come again to your village in health, you will all admit that your gods have no power over me, and that I am protected by the true and living Jehovah God!'

All that week the sacred men did their very best to kill John. Each day he would hear the conches being sounded, as the sacred men called on their gods to help them kill him. The islanders were very curious to see what would happen to him. People kept coming from all over the island to see for themselves if he was still alive and asking him if he felt ill at all.

When John arrived at the village the next Lord's Day he found a large crowd waiting. When he appeared many of the islanders looked at each other as if to ask, 'Can it really be Missi, alive and well?' After greeting them all, John turned to the sacred men and challenged them to admit that they had failed to kill him by their sorcery. They had to acknowledge that this was so, but when he asked why they had failed, they made the excuse that John was himself a sacred man who had a God who was more powerful than the ones they served.

John agreed that his God was indeed stronger than theirs and went on, 'He protected me, and helped me; for he is the only living and true God, the only God that can hear or answer any prayer… Your gods cannot hear prayers, but my God can and will hear and answer you, if you will give heart and life to him, and love and serve him only. This is my God, and he is also your friend if you will hear and follow his voice.'

With these words John sat down on a fallen tree-trunk and invited the natives to gather round him while he talked to them about the love and mercy of his God and told them how to worship and please him. Many of the people, including two of the sacred men, sat down and listened very carefully as John explained to them that they were sinners who needed to be saved through faith in the Lord Jesus Christ.

Suddenly the third of the sacred men came up brandishing his spear and made straight for John with the intention of thrusting it through him. Turning to the people sitting around him, John said, 'Of course he can kill me with his spear, but he undertook to kill me by Nahak or sorcery, and promised not to use against me any weapons of war; and if you let him kill me now, you will kill your friend, one who lives among you and only tries to do you good, as you all know so well. I know that if you kill me thus, my God will be angry and will punish you.'

The sacred man was very angry with the people for listening to John and he leapt about, waving his spear and shouting. However, most of the people, including the other two sacred men, were on John's side. They all crowded close around him, so the man did not dare throw his spear.

For weeks afterwards that sacred man followed John around, every now and again suddenly appearing on the path in front of him brandishing his huge spear. However, God continued to protect John and he was able to go about his work unharmed.

After this the other two sacred men were very friendly to John and the Christian teachers and actually tried to help them in their work. They even escorted John — one of them walking in front of him and the other behind, both with their clubs and spears at the ready to protect him — when he went to talk to some of the warriors who were involved in yet another bout of fighting.

The failure of the sacred men to kill John by their sorcery did help to shake the islanders' faith in the power of their priests, but they had such a deep-seated fear of the sacred men and their sorcery that even those who were eventually converted could never quite shake off all their superstitious fears about the dreaded Nahak.

All this time Mr and Mrs Mathieson were still working at the other mission station on the south-west side of the island. Neither of them was in good health, but they were keen to carry on their work of teaching the natives from God's Word. John used to visit them from time to time and on one occasion they sent him a message asking if he could let them have some flour as their food supply was running low.

As there was a war raging at the time it was too dangerous to try to cross the island on foot. The sea was far too rough for John to use his mission boat, so he asked Chief Nowar and Manuman, one of the two sacred men who had become friendly after their unsuccessful attempt to kill him, if they could get some of their men to take him to the Mathiesons' home by canoe. He found a large pot with a closely-fitting lid, which he filled with flour and fastened this securely in the middle of the canoe. They tied other packages round their bodies so that they would not be swept away in the rough seas.

Soon all the men in the canoe, including John, were thoroughly drenched with the spray from the surf. However, it was when they reached a spot a couple of miles from the Mathiesons' home that the going became really difficult. The waves breaking on the reef were so huge that the men said they could not paddle any further and would have to attempt a landing. John felt sure that the canoe would be smashed to pieces, but the crew waited till they saw one of the smaller waves coming, then paddled with all their might. The canoe rose high in the air on the crest of the wave and all except John were thrown out. However, the natives were all good swimmers and when John, who could not swim, leapt out of the boat, one of the men grabbed hold of him and helped him to land. Meanwhile, Manuman clung on to the canoe until some of the others swam out and helped him drag it in to the shore. John was relieved to see one of them striding through the waves, balancing the precious pot of flour on his head and even more so when he discovered that the contents were still dry!

Once safely on land, John parted from his companions, who were going to wait for the next suitable tide. Praising God for protecting them and keeping them all safe, John set off on foot for the Mathiesons' home, with one of the local men carrying the pot of flour for him.

After spending a few hours with his friends, John left for home, intending this time to cross the island on foot. He did not dare stay away any longer in case thieves broke into his house while it was empty and stole all his possessions.

As the sun was about to set, John could not find any natives who were willing to accompany him on his journey. They were sure he would be killed. But John knew that it would be completely dark by the time he reached the areas where the tribes lived who were most likely to attack him. They would not be roaming about the island at night because all the islanders were afraid of the dark and rarely left their villages after nightfall. Provided he kept well away from the villages, he thought the risk would not be too great.

So John set out alone, walking along the seashore as quickly as he could — even running at times. If he heard voices approaching he would slip in among the trees, where he could not be seen, until the men had passed. He had to follow the shore as closely as he could, or he would have lost his way.

After some time he came to a place where the path climbed almost vertically up a high rock, with a sheer drop to the sea roaring far below if he missed his footing in the dark. With a silent prayer to the Lord for help, John began climbing, pullling himself up by grabbing hold of tree roots and using bushes to prevent himself from falling when he needed to stop for a rest.

When he reached the top he had to crawl a distance along the very edge of the cliff to avoid being seen from one of the villages. Then he came to a deep ravine which he had to follow inland for some distance, away from the shore, until he found a place where it was safe to cross. Missing the place where he had meant to turn back to the shore, he came to a spot where he could see the glow of fires and hear voices. He realized he was near one of the villages where the natives were not friendly to the missionaries, so he quietly draw back among the trees and, now that he knew where he was, made his way back towards the shore.

When he reached the cliffs, he could not find the path down to the shore in the dark. He hunted for a while, but eventually decided he would have to try to slide down the rocks, which were fairly smooth at that place. He knew that at high tide it would be dangerous to attempt this, so he tried dropping stones and even his umbrella into the water. He then listened, trying to tell from the splash how deep the water was, but the sea was so far below that he could hear nothing. However, to wait until daylight would have meant almost certain death from the hostile tribesmen, so, trusting himself to God, he lay down on the rock with his feet straight out in front of him and let go. He felt himself rushing very swiftly downhill and a few moments later landed safely in shallow water. He jumped to his feet, praising the Lord Jesus for keeping him safe, picked up his dropped umbrella and set off once more along the shore path.

After that the going was easy, but just before he reached home there was another dangerous moment, when he met a group of young men armed with muskets. At first they mistook him for an enemy and were just about to shoot him when he called out, 'I am Missi! Don't shoot; my love to you, my friends!' He then offered them a gift of fish-hooks if they would show him the shortest way back to his mission station. This they were very ready to do.

Having arrived safely home, John thanked God for keeping him safe and then went to bed for a well-earned sleep.

The next day when the local natives heard that John had walked all the way from the other side of the island in the dark, they exclaimed, 'Surely any of us would have been killed! Your Jehovah God alone thus protects you and brings you safely home.'

To those words John heartily agreed saying, 'Yes! And he will be your protector and helper too, if only you will obey and trust him.'

John himself said afterwards that he could not have faced either the outward journey by canoe or the walk back through the bush in darkness, had it not been for the assurance in his heart that he was doing the work the Lord wanted him to do and that the Lord Jesus Christ would take care of him. Once again he was assured of the truth of the words of the apostle Paul: 'I can do all things through Christ who strengthens me.'

To think about

We read that Nowar and some of the other islanders introduced family worship. If you are a member of a Christian family have a think about the worship conducted in your family, because the short time set aside to meet together as a family in prayer and reading the Scriptures is one of the most important uses of time.

Many Christians testify to the way in which God used family worship times to lead them to Christ.

There are a number of good books available for use in family worship times. I would urge all Christian parents to buy some of these and make use of them, always praying that God might bless your spiritual activities to the soul of each member of your family. Read the command given to the Israelites in Deuteronomy 6:6-9. They have application to God's people in this generation — and maybe today more than ever. I trust that all parents will not neglect this important duty.

12.
Measles and hurricanes

One day, when John had been living on Tanna for nearly two years, a ship arrived in the harbour bringing two new mission workers to the island. They were a young Canadian couple, Samuel and Elizabeth Johnston. It was the rainy season when they landed and while they were waiting for their own mission station to be built they stayed with John as his guests. Their companionship was just what John needed in his lonely situation. It was good to have the opportunity to talk about the Lord with other Christians. No doubt the three of them often prayed to the Lord pleading with him to work in the hearts of the islanders and bring them out of the darkness of paganism and into the kingdom of the Lord Jesus Christ.

One of the first things the Johnstons had to learn was the local language. Every day John would teach them fourteen or fifteen new words to learn by heart. Then they would try to hold conversations in the Tannese language, using the words they already knew, to see how well they could make themselves understood. In this way they made rapid progress and were soon able to help John in his work among the natives.

But trouble was brewing once more. One morning three or four trading ships sailed into the harbour and dropped anchor. One of the captains came to see John and confidently told him,

'We know how to bring down your proud Tannese now! We'll humble them before you!'

John was horrified. 'Surely you don't mean to attack and destroy these poor people?' he asked, imagining that they meant to invade the island with guns blazing, killing the natives and driving the ones remaining out of their homes. But the men had found a much more devious means of bringing death and destruction to the islanders.

They had landed four young men on different parts of the island, all of whom were ill with measles, in a deliberate attempt to spread the infection among the native people. (Diseases brought in from outside, such as measles, were often deadly to the natives, who had not been exposed to the infection from childhood like most Europeans, and so had no resistance to it.) The cruel traders quite unashamedly declared their intention to kill off the natives so that white people could take over their land! John was deeply shocked and told them plainly what he thought of their behaviour, but it made no impression on them.

As well as landing the infected men on the island, the traders invited Kapuku, a young chief who was a friend of Mr and Mrs Mathieson, to go on board one of their ships, promising him a present if he did. However, as soon as he arrived on board the crew seized him and shut him up in the ship's hold with a group of natives who had the measles. They left him there for a whole day, without any food, and then put him ashore a long way from home, without giving him the gift they had promised. Weak and hungry as he was, he eventually found his way back to his village, taking the dreaded disease back with him.

The sickness spread among the population like wildfire, often affecting whole villages at a time so that there was no one left to look after those who were ill. John and the Johnstons went round the villages every day, taking medicines and food and drinking water to those who were ill. Many of those whom they helped recovered, but in all almost a third of the population died.

Some of the natives were so hot from the fever which accompanied the measles that they ran into the sea for relief. However, the shock of the cold water caused many of them to collapse and drown. Others dug beds in the cool earth and covered themselves with the soil, but often that was the very spot where they died. They had literally dug their own graves.

Thirteen of John's helpers from Aneityum died and the rest packed up and prepared to go home. As they were standing waiting to board the mission boat, the *John Knox*, to sail home to Aneityum, John went up to Abraham, the old teacher who had been his most loyal friend and companion, and asked him, 'Are you also going to leave me here alone on Tanna, to fight the battles of the Lord?'

Abraham had evidently thought John was leaving too and asked with some surprise, 'Missi, will you remain?'

John replied that he could not leave the Lord's work, but he realized that both their lives would be in great danger if they stayed. Though he had hoped Abraham would stay with him, he would not ask him to do so because of the threat to his life.

After he had thought about it for a while, and when he saw John was determined to stay, Abraham said, 'Then, Missi, I remain with you of my own free choice, and with all my heart. We will live and die together in the work of the Lord. I will never leave you while you are spared on Tanna.' Saying that, he picked up the box in which he had packed his belongings, swung it onto his shoulder and took it back into his house.

John knew that he and his companions would now be in great danger because the islanders would blame them for the disaster that had come upon them, even though it was in fact the traders who had brought the infection and spread it among the people, while John and his friends had only tried to help them. As far as the natives were concerned, they were all white men and it was the white men who were to blame for the deadly disease.

One evening, after a time of prayer with John and Abraham, Samuel and Elizabeth Johnston were about to go to their own rooms for the night when they found two armed men hanging about outside the house. The men were carrying huge clubs and their faces were hidden by warpaint. When John went out to see what they wanted they said, 'Medicine for a sick boy.' However, they were obviously reluctant to come in and get it. From the strange way they were behaving and the fact that they had tried to disguise themselves, John soon guessed that they had really come to kill the missionaries.

John prepared the medicine they had asked for, keeping an eye on them as he did so. When it was ready, he tried to give it to them, but they would not take it and instead brandished their weapons. Showing them the door, John told them, 'You see that Mr Johnston is now leaving, and you too must leave this room for tonight. Tomorrow, you can bring the boy or come for the medicine.' They still hesitated, but John insisted and they turned to leave.

Mr Johnston had gone out of the door first, but he stooped down to pick up a little kitten which had run out while the door was left open. As he did so one of the natives aimed a blow at him with his club. Mr Johnson ducked to avoid the blow but fell to the ground and was only saved from another attack by John's two dogs, who leapt at the two men, barking fiercely.

When John rushed out to see what was happening the two men turned on him with their clubs, but again the dogs leapt into the attack and one of them suffered a blow from a club that had been intended for John. When John set the dogs on them, the attackers finally ran off, as John shouted after them, 'Remember, Jehovah God sees you and will punish you for trying to murder his servants.' As the two men fled, they were followed by a large number of other natives who had evidently been hanging about in the bush hoping to join in looting the mission buildings. Once more John was reminded of the Lord's promise: 'Lo! I am with you always.'

John had by now become used to living under the threat of death and when all was quiet that night he went to bed as usual and slept soundly. However, Mr Johnston was so shaken by the attack that he could not sleep at all. For the next couple of weeks he continued to accompany John as he went round the villages visiting the sick, but he still could not sleep at night and eventually asked John for some medicine to help him sleep. When he fell ill a few days later John and Elizabeth at first thought it was the effects of the medicine, but they discovered he had contracted tetanus from a wound which had become infected.

John was suffering from another attack of malarial fever at that time and was so weak that he could not walk unaided, but for the next two days he and Elizabeth nursed Samuel with loving care. The sick man's teeth were so tightly clamped together from the tetanus that they had to use a knife, a spoon and pieces of wood to force them apart so that they could give him the medicine he needed. Then they kept him awake by repeatedly splashing his face with cold water and moving him about. For a time he seemed a little better, but he suffered a relapse and died. Just three weeks after the attack outside John's house, John and Elizabeth sadly laid Samuel Johnston's body to rest in a grave close to the mission house, beside that of John's dear wife Mary and their baby son, Peter.

Elizabeth Johnston soon afterwards returned to Aneityum, where she taught for nearly three years at the girls' school run by Dr Geddie and his wife. She later married John's good friend Joseph Copeland and moved with him to the island of Fotuna, where she was to spend the rest of her life helping her new husband win the natives to faith in Christ.

Samuel Johnston's death came as a great blow to John, for the two men had got on extremely well together and he greatly missed his friend and helper. However, he took comfort from the knowledge that, as in the case of his wife Mary, he was 'not lost ... only gone before' to be with the Lord. He was soon to lose another Christian friend and helper, too.

A few years earlier a young chief from Tanna named Kowia had gone to live in Aneityum and had been converted there. He married a Christian girl from Aneityum and they had two children. Some time before the outbreak of measles he returned to Tanna with his family to work with John as one of the Christian teachers on the island. He and his family lived with John at the mission and he was a great help to John and Abraham.

The islanders tried to persuade Kowia to give up his Christian faith and to leave the mission. When they failed to do so they threatened to take away his lands and to deprive him of his rank as a chief. However, nothing would make him disown his Lord or abandon John. 'Take all!' he told them. 'I shall still stand by Missi and the worship of Jehovah.'

One day a group of natives arrived selling fowls, and Kowia bought some for the mission. Then they tried to steal the birds back and offered them to John for sale, hoping to be paid for them twice over. Seeing what was happening, Kowia called out, 'Don't purchase these, Missi! I have just bought them for you, and paid for them!' At that the men turned on Kowia, mocking him and calling him a coward.

Kowia stood up to his full height and, looking round at the watching crowd, turned to John and said, 'Missi, they think that because I am now a Christian I have become a coward, a woman, to bear every abuse and insult they can heap upon me! But I will show them for once that I am no coward, that I am still their chief, and that Christianity does not take away but gives us courage and nerve!'

Then he grabbed a huge club from one of the warriors standing nearby, swung it above his head and challenged them: 'Come any of you, come all against your chief! My Jehovah God makes my heart and arms strong. He will help me in this battle as he helps me in other things, for he inspires me to show you that Christians are no cowards, though they are men of peace. Come on, and you will yet know that I am Kowia your chief.'

As he moved towards them, the men who had been taunting him all turned and ran off. Handing back the club to its owner, Kowia asked, 'Where are the cowards now?' After that he had no more trouble from the natives.

Soon after Mr Johnston's death John became very ill and was lovingly cared for by Abraham and Kowia. One day he woke up and found Kowia at his bedside. 'Missi,' Kowia said, 'all our Aneityumese are sick. Missi Johnston is dead. You are very sick, and I am weak and dying. Alas, when I too am dead, who will climb the tree and get you a coconut to drink? And who will bathe your lips and brow?'

Kowia burst into tears as he continued: 'Missi, the Tanna-men hate us all on account of the worship of Jehovah; and now I fear he is going to take away all his servants from this land, and leave my people to the Evil One and his service!'

John was too weak to reply, but he listened as Kowia prayed. He began by speaking about the death of Mr Johnston and the fact that all the other Christians on the island were ill, including Kowia himself. Then he asked, 'O Lord, our Father in heaven, are you going to take away all your servants, and your worship from this dark land? What do you mean to do, O Lord? The Tannese hate you and your worship and your servants; but surely, O Lord, you cannot forsake Tanna and leave our people to die in the darkness! Oh, make the hearts of this people soft to your Word and sweet to your worship; teach them to fear and love Jesus; and oh, restore and spare Missi, dear Missi Paton, that Tanna may be saved!' John was very touched to hear these words coming from the lips of a man who had once been a cannibal and worshipped idols.

Some days later Kowia came to see John once more and told him, 'Missi, I am very weak; I am dying. I come to bid you farewell, and go away to die...' While John had been ill, Kowia's wife and children had all fallen ill and died and he spoke of his wish to be buried beside them. 'I am happy, looking to Jesus!' he told John, and urged the missionary to pray again for his poor people who were still in the darkness of heathenism and hated the Lord and his worship. His last words to John were: 'Farewell, Missi... we will meet again in Jesus and with Jesus!'

In the days following the deadly outbreak of measles, the traders who had been responsible for introducing the disease to the island tried to put the blame for it on the missionaries, in order to save themselves from the anger of the islanders. Some of them threatened not to trade with the natives, or to supply them with the things they desperately wanted, such as tobacco and ammunition for their guns, unless they killed or drove away John and his helper, Abraham.

There were other troubles, too. Early in 1861, when the inhabitants were still recovering from the effects of the measles epidemic, the island was swept with severe storms, which uprooted huge trees, tossing them about and smashing them to pieces like so many bits of straw, and destroying most of the island's crops. Coconut palms and fruit trees were torn down and half-ripe fruit and bananas left strewn all over the ground. Whole villages of native huts were flattened in the rough seas and canoes were smashed to pieces on the coral reefs.

John's house was badly damaged, with only one room left standing. The new church, which had cost him so much hard work to build, was almost levelled to the ground. On the other side of the island, the Mathiesons' home was also badly damaged and they too could only use one room. In spite of the torrential rain John had to stand guard over his house, because otherwise the natives would have looted the damaged building and stolen everything he owned.

Soon after this the war-chief Miaki's baby son died. As part of their pagan funeral rites, the natives murdered four of their own men so that their spirits could accompany the dead child's spirit into the next world where, the superstitious islanders believed, they would act as his servants. Then they threatened to kill John and his friends as well. For four days armed warriors surrounded what was left of John's house, while he and his companions locked themselves in the one room left standing after the storm and prayed to the Lord to keep them safe. The men broke down the fences around John's plantation, cut down the few bananas left on the trees after the storm and destroyed them. They also killed his fowls and several of his goats, which were his only supply of milk.

In the following months there were several new cases of cannibalism and reports that as many as thirteen or fourteen people, mainly refugees or prisoners of war, had been killed and eaten. The missionaries' teaching had evidently had some effect, because when two dead bodies were offered as a gift to the villagers who lived nearest to the mission the local people refused them, saying, 'Now we know that it is wrong to kill and eat our fellow-creatures.' But they did not seem to see anything wrong in giving the bodies of men who had been killed in war to other tribes to eat, in exchange for wild pigs, which were only found in the centre of the island.

Even Chief Nowar became afraid. His life had been threatened because of his friendship with the missionaries. He urged John to escape from the island (which would have meant a voyage of over fifty miles on the open sea in John's small boat, without the help of any experienced sailors!). When John refused, Nowar stopped attending the worship services and went back to dressing and acting like a pagan for a few weeks, until he thought the immediate danger was over.

Following all the deaths from the measles and destruction caused by the hurricanes, there was a severe thunderstorm in which lightning struck and killed a man and woman as well as setting off a landslide. The natives saw this as a sign from their tribal gods that they were angry with the islanders for allowing the missionaries to live among them and teach the worship of the Christian God. So the danger for John and his companions was greater than ever.

To think about

Chief Nowar went back to his old sinful ways for a time when the going became difficult. He feared the other chiefs and the people of the island. In the parable of the sower Christ spoke of such 'turn-coats' (Matthew 13:1-9, 18-23).

There is always the danger that those who return to the world will stay there and there is no salvation for those who do. Christ, the Saviour, is to be found in the church. He is the Head of the church and worldly people have no part in that glorious organization, sometimes described as the Bride of Christ. Read Hebrews 10:26-39 and there you will find a most severe warning to all who are thinking of going back to their godless, worldly way of life.

One mark of a true Christian is faithfulness to the very end of life. Does that describe you?

13.
A man-of-war comes to Tanna

Tanna was not the only island which had been struck by the measles epidemic or the storms. On the nearby island of Erromanga, where the Rev. George Gordon and his wife Ellen had been missionaries for the last four years, the islanders blamed the missionaries and the Christian worship they had introduced for the disasters they had suffered. The sandalwood traders actually encouraged them in this, because they hated the missionaries who condemned their evil ways as well as the trade in weapons. They were also anxious to save their own lives by throwing the blame for the measles, which they had introduced, onto someone else.

One day while George Gordon was busy thatching a roof for the hut which was to house his printing-press, he sent the young men who were helping him to fetch something he needed. While they were gone, a group of warriors, who had been hiding in the bush watching and waiting for an opportunity to catch him by himself, came up to the missionary asking him to go back to the mission house with them as they needed medicine for a sick boy. They insisted he lead the way and, as they were all crossing a stream, the warriors struck Mr Gordon from behind with their tomahawks and killed him.

Hearing a lot of shouting, Mrs Gordon came out of the house and asked, 'What's the cause of all that noise?'

George and Ellen Gordon

'Oh, nothing!' one of the natives told her. 'Only the boys amusing themselves!'

'Where are the boys?', she then wanted to know. As she turned round to look, the man who had just spoken to her attacked her from behind and killed her too.

One night soon after this, a boat belonging to one of the traders brought over a party of Erromangan warriors to Tanna, where they urged the local chiefs to kill the missionaries, as they had done, and so sweep away the worship of the Christian God from the islands.

The next day a crowd of armed men came to John's mission station and threatened that if no man-of-war came to punish the Erromangans for killing their missionaries, then they too would unite to kill the missionaries and drive out the worship of the Christian God from Tanna. One chief called out in a loud voice, for John to hear, 'My love to the Erromangans! They are strong and brave men...! They have killed their Missi and his wife, while we only talk about it. They have destroyed the worship and driven away Jehovah!'

That night the islanders held a festival at which they celebrated the murder and praised the people of Erromanga. Once again John's friend Chief Nowar put on his warpaint and started going about armed with bow and arrows and tomahawk like a pagan warrior. He warned John: 'If they are not punished

for what has been done on Erromanga, nothing else can keep
them here from killing you and me and all who worship at the
mission house!'

Nowar was very worried and even began to express
doubts about God and the Christian faith. 'How is it that
Jehovah did not protect the Gordons and the Erromangan
worshippers?' he asked. 'If the Erromangans are not punished, neither will our Tannese be punished, though they
murder all Jehovah's people!'

However, Abraham, the old Christian teacher from Aneityum, remained loyal to John and stood by him at all times, in
spite of the danger. They used to hold family worship together,
taking it in turns to lead. The night after the news of the murder
and the threats to their own lives Abraham prayed: 'O Lord,
our heavenly Father, they have murdered your servants on
Erromanga. They have banished the Aneityumese from dark
Tanna. And now they want to kill Missi Paton and me! Our
great King, protect us, and make their hearts soft and sweet to
your worship. Or, if they are permitted to kill us ... wash us in
the blood of your dear Son Jesus Christ. He came down to earth
and shed his blood for sinners; through him forgive us our sins
and take us to heaven... Our Lord, our hearts are pained just
now, and we weep over the death of your dear servants; but
make our hearts good and strong for your cause, and take away
all our fears. Make us two and all your servants strong for you
and for your worship; and if they kill us two, let us die together
in your good work, like your servants Missi Gordon the man
and Missi Gordon the woman.'

Soon after this Miaki, the war-chief, came to John's house,
accompanied by several of his men. 'You and the worship are
the cause of all the sickness and death now taking place on
Tanna!' he accused John. He claimed that the people of
Erromanga were all well now that they had killed the missionaries and said, 'The worship is killing us all... We hate the

worship. We must kill you and it, and we shall all be well again.'

Miaki then sent a message to some of the chiefs on the other side of the island, encouraging them to kill Mr and Mrs Mathieson. He also urged his men to steal all John's possessions. They managed to catch and kill one of his two watch-dogs, which they ate at one of their feasts.

Then, on a bright, sunny morning, the trading-ship *Blue Bell* sailed into the harbour and cast anchor. The captain and mate came ashore as they were bringing letters for John. On landing, they were immediately surrounded by a ring of armed natives who pointed weapons at them and threatened to kill them if they made the slightest move. The islanders then called John and told him, 'This is one of the vessels which brought the measles. You and they made the sickness, and destroyed our people. Now, if you do not leave with this vessel, we will kill you all.'

John realized that they wanted to frighten him into boarding the ship in a hurry, so they could loot the house and steal everything he had left behind. He told them, 'I will not leave you; I cannot leave you in this way; and if you murder these men or me, Jehovah will punish you.' Then he reminded them how he had given them medicine, knives, axes, blankets and clothes, and had never done any of them any harm. He warned them that if they killed the two traders, the other men on the ship would punish them before they sailed and that when the news got around the white men would send a man-of-war to burn their villages.

John hustled the two traders into a boat and told them to return to their ship as quickly as they could while he continued to distract the natives' attention by arguing with them. When Miaki complained that his medicine had killed all the people, John told him that this was simply not true: 'My medicine with God's blessing saved many lives. You know well that all who followed my rules recovered from the measles... Now you seek to kill me for saving your lives and the lives of your people!'

Turning to one of the chiefs standing by, whose name was Yorian, John appealed to him as a witness. Yorian had at one time been ill, almost at the point of death, when John had given him medicine. Had that medicine saved his life? Yorian was forced to admit, Yes, it had.

By now the two traders had got into their boat and Miaki shouted to his men, 'Let them go! Don't kill them today!' Then he called out to the traders: 'Come on shore and trade with us tomorrow.'

The next day the traders came back but the natives quickly surrounded their boat, waving clubs and tomahawks. Then, at the last moment, Miaki lost his nerve, remembering John's words the previous day. He called out to his men to stop, because 'Missi said that, if we kill them a man-of-war will come and take revenge on us.'

The sailors quickly pushed their boat off the shore and beat a hasty retreat to the *Blue Bell*, but not before the islanders had grabbed hold of the captain's Newfoundland dog in the scuffle. When the ship sailed the next day, the dog was left behind because none of the sailors dared venture on shore to get it back.

In his frustration at letting the traders get away, Miaki then wanted to kill John and Abraham, but this time Chief Nowar stood up for them and once again their lives were spared.

After that John woke up on several occasions during the night to find that thieves were trying to break into his house. Often it was his dog Clutha who woke him up by barking, or by tugging at the bedclothes till he woke up. If John let her out to chase the thieves, they would all run away very quickly. Another time they ran off when John shouted out at them from inside the house.

However, not all the islanders were as hostile towards John, or as warlike, as Miaki and his men. Many of the people were so exhausted and weak as a result of the measles epidemic and the shortage of food caused by the dreadful storms that they did not really want to fight any wars for a time. Several of the chiefs from another part of the island came to see John and after a long talk promised to try to stop Miaki's attempts to start another war. John gave them each a knife and fork and a tin plate before they left.

Then a man came to see him with a nasty cut on his hand which had been bitten by a fish. John gave him some first aid and put a dressing on the cut so that it healed up without any trouble. The man then went away and told everyone how the missionary had helped him.

John was also able to help the islanders with their fishing. The women and girls of some of the inland tribes were very skilful at weaving nets, using fibre made from the bark of local trees. John arranged for one of these tribes to make him a huge fishing-net. He then let each of the local tribes borrow it for a few days at a time. With this large net they were able to catch so many fish that they had enough to trade some with the inland tribes in exchange for wild pigs or other animals which they had caught. In this way they were able to make up for the shortage of food caused by the hurricanes which had destroyed their crops and fruit trees.

So, for a time, the islanders were more friendly towards John. He had no trouble in finding men to work for him at laying the foundations for a new church building, which was to replace the one destroyed in the storms. They put up new fences for him and repaired the mission buildings. John paid them for their work with knives, axes and lengths of calico. As they worked he had plenty of opportunities to speak to them about the Lord and how to worship and serve him.

Miaki was very angry when he realized what was happening. He tried to stop the people working for John or being taught by him. One day John arrived home just in time to put out a fire which some of Miaki's men had lit under the verandah of his house, hoping to burn the house down. Another time one of Miaki's cousins sold John a poisonous fish, telling him it was good to eat, but Chief Nowar saw it in time and warned John not to eat it.

In spite of Miaki's threats even more people kept coming to work for John and to be taught by him. In all about sixty people, including several members of Miaki's own family, attended the services he held each Lord's Day and every Wednesday afternoon.

John and Abraham also taught classes in the mission school where John offered a red shirt as a prize to the first chief who learnt the whole alphabet by heart and could repeat it without a mistake. The prize was won by an Inikahi chief who then started trying to teach other people the names of the letters like this: 'A is a man's legs with the body cut off; ...C is a three-quarters moon;... E is a man with one club under his feet and another over his head...' and so on. 'I have taught my little child, who can scarcely walk, the names of them all,' the chief told his listeners. 'You will soon learn to read the book, if you try it with all your heart!'

But all this time Miaki was still trying to make trouble for John. He and his men started threatening him again, claiming that traders would not come to the island while he was there. Even Nowar seemed to be taking Miaki's side and threatened: 'Miaki will make a great wind and sink any man-of-war that comes here. We will take the man-of-war and kill all that are on board. If you and Abraham do not leave us we will kill you both, for we must have the traders and the powder.'

Just then the mission ship *John Knox* was sighted coming in to harbour, followed by two large battleships, or men-of war.

John turned to the crowd and challenged them: 'Now is your time! Make all possible haste! Let Miaki raise his great wind now; get all your men ready; I will tell them that you mean to fight, and you will find them always ready!'

At that Miaki's men ran off in terror. Nowar came up to John and said, 'Missi, I know that my talk is all lies, but if I speak the truth, they will kill me.'

John told him to trust in God, who had sent the ships to protect them from being murdered, but Nowar was still afraid and he kept out of the way all the time the British ships were in the harbour.

Meanwhile people came flocking from all over the island to see the big ships.

The two captains came on shore, with Dr Geddie from the mission, and asked John what was happening on the island. When he told them about the threats against his life, they offered to take him to Aneityum or some other place where he would be safe. However, John was certain that if he left the island he would not be able to return and it would be the end of the mission work there. How could he leave the people, especially when he knew that all the islanders who had been friendly to him or attended services at the mission would be singled out for punishment once he had gone?

The captains had a meeting with the island chiefs and extracted a promise from Miaki and his men that they would not harm John. One of the local chiefs, Nouka, explained the problem: 'We love Missi. But when the traders tell us that the worship makes us sick, and when they bribe us with tobacco and powder to kill him or drive him away, some believe them and our hearts do bad conduct to Missi.'

Then the chiefs were invited on board one of the battleships where they saw all the troops drawn up in ranks, ready for action, and watched as one of the huge cannons was fired. They were impressed at the time, but the effects quickly wore off once the ships had sailed away out of sight. When the islanders saw that no action was taken to punish the islanders of Erromanga for the murder of their missionaries, they soon went back to their old ways. There were more threats against John's life and even Nowar boasted that he was free to do as he liked, as he had not been present at the meeting with the British captains, and so he was not bound by any promises to them.

To think about

What was happening on the island of Tanna is described in Psalm 2. The rulers of the earth are conspiring to get rid of the gospel from the face of the earth. They crucified Christ and want to do the same to his followers. Read this psalm, for there we are told that God sits in heaven and laughs at the fruitless efforts of weak, sinful men. For a time the heathens of Tanna appeared to have the victory, but today the church is alive and active in Vanuatu. Men and women there have 'kissed the Son' and so made peace with God.

Miaki was the ring-leader of opposition to John, and others followed. Today it is just the same. Powerful, godless leaders fight against God's people and usually have many followers. Think of the action of the godless rulers of the former USSR and the way Christians were persecuted under that regime. But Christ has the victory and the Day of Judgement will show this to be completely true. Where do you and your family stand in this great cosmic battle? May you be able to say with godly Joshua, 'But as for me and my house, we will serve the Lord' (Joshua 24:15).

14.
The last straw

War was in the air again. The people could talk of nothing else and groups of armed men stood around in the villages, all waiting for something to happen. All the old grudges and rivalries came to the surface and John and his helpers found themselves at the centre of the arguments.

One of the inland chiefs, called Ian, who wanted John to stay, spoke up for him. Miaki and Nouka then said, 'If you will keep Missi and his worship, take him with you to your own land, for we will not have him to live at the harbour.'

Ian leapt to his feet and shouted angrily, 'On whose land does the Missi live, yours or ours? Who fight against the worship and all good, who are the thieves and murderers, who tell the lies — you or we?' He went on to remind Miaki and the others that the land which John had bought to build his mission station had originally been the property of the inland tribes. 'The land was not yours to sell,' he told them. 'It was really ours. Your fathers stole it from us long ago by war; but we would not have asked it back, had you not asked us to take Missi away. Now we will defend him on it, and he will teach us and our people in our own land!'

It was Chief Ian himself who came to fetch John to attend the next meeting of the chiefs and warriors. John did not want to go, and sent a message begging them not to go to war on his account, but Ian insisted: 'Missi, come with me, come now!'

When they arrived at the village square, John found the two parties of armed warriors drawn up facing each other across the open space — Ian's men, carrying muskets as well as their spears and clubs on one side, and Miaki, Nouka and their men on the other, looking as if they were terrified of what was going to happen.

Ian marched into the centre of the square and, turning to John, pointed out the two groups: 'Missi, these are my men and your friends! We are met to defend you and the worship... These are your enemies and ours! ... Missi, say the word, and the muskets of my men will sweep all opposition away and the worship will spread and we will all be strong for it on Tanna.'

But John could only give one answer: '... I am here to teach you how to turn away from all wickedness, to worship and serve Jehovah, and to live in peace. How can I approve of any person being killed for me or for the worship? My God would be angry at me and punish me, if I did!'

Ian warned him, 'Then ... you will be murdered and the worship destroyed.' But John stepped into the middle of the circle of armed warriors and spoke loudly for them all to hear: 'You may shoot or murder me, but I am your best friend. I am not afraid to die. You will only send me the sooner to my Jehovah God, whom I love and serve, and to my dear Saviour Jesus Christ, who died for me and for you, and who sent me here to tell you all about his love...' He went on to urge them to leave their evil ways and to serve the true God and love him. Then he warned that if they killed him, God would punish them in his own time and way.

Chief Ian was not satisfied. 'Missi, they will kill you!' he said. 'They will kill us, and you will be to blame!'

But Miaki and Nouka seized the opportunity to avoid a fight which they could well lose, and shouted, 'Missi's word is good! Let us all obey it. Let us all worship.'

Sirawia, one of Ian's supporters, then spoke up and said that if Miaki and his men would let John live in peace on the land which he had bought, then there would be peace. If not, the inland tribes would fight to regain the land which had been taken from them by Miaki's people. Gifts of food were then exchanged as peace-offerings.

For a short time after this meeting of the tribes John and his helpers were allowed to carry on with their work undisturbed. However, Miaki and Nouka were still out to make trouble with the inland tribes. After a time they announced publicly that they were going to kill Ian by their sorcery, the dreaded Nahak. Ian in fact did become ill soon afterwards, but John treated him and he seemed to improve for a while. When Ian fell ill again John suspected that someone was poisoning him. Believing their chief was dying, Ian's followers turned against John, blaming him and saying this would never have happened if he had let them kill Miaki and his men.

One day a group of men led by Ian's brother came to fetch John to visit Ian. When they reached Ian's house John quickly found himself left alone with the sick man and suspected a trap.

Ian appeared to be very ill, probably dying, and he asked John, 'Come near me, and sit by my bedside to talk with me.'

John sat down beside him and began to speak, but suddenly Ian pulled out a large knife which he had hidden beside his bed and pointed it straight at John's heart. John sat unable to move or speak, but he urgently sent up silent prayers to the Lord as he waited for Ian's next move. A few moments passed, which must have seemed a very long time. Then Ian suddenly swung the knife away, and told John, 'Go, go quickly!'

John stood up and left the hut. He walked very quietly in case anyone was watching, although the place seemed deserted. When he was out of sight of the village, he ran for his life.

Evidently there had been a plot that Ian should kill John while they were alone together, in the knowledge that by the time anyone came to make enquiries the chief would be dead.

If a British man-of-war came there would be no witnesses to the crime and no murderer for them to arrest, because he would be dead anyway.

Ian died soon afterwards. According to the native customs his two wives were also killed and the three bodies were taken out to sea in a canoe and then sunk.

Miaki was triumphant. He had killed his enemy by sorcery! He boasted that he would call up a great wind from the sea to destroy the homes and crops of all his enemies. Not long afterwards, there really was a storm which laid everything waste on the side of the island where Ian's people lived. Sirawia and others had been clamouring for revenge on Miaki ever since Ian's death. The destruction of their houses and crops was the last straw. War broke out between the two sides.

John and Abraham were told by both sides that if they kept to the mission house they would not be harmed. However, they soon found that their house was in the very thick of the fighting, as Miaki and his men used it to shelter from the enemy's guns. Bullets were flying all around the house, while the bush on all sides echoed to the blood-curdling war-cries uttered by the warriors.

As the fighting went on, old Chief Nowar came to John's aid, but he received a spear-wound in the knee and his men carried him off home amid wild shouts of triumph.

When Nowar was gone, the attackers smashed their way into the mission buildings, where they broke open boxes and tore up books, scattering everything about. They then made off with John's boat and anything else they could lay their hands on.

While this was going on, John and his companions were locked in a bedroom. The men began firing their guns into the room and trying to break down the door. One of the chiefs called to John, pretending to be sorry for him, but when he came to the window to answer, the man shouted, 'Come on, let us kill him now!' and a tomahawk came whizzing in through the opening, aimed at John's head.

When John tried to stop them with warnings of punishment by God or the British navy, the men took no notice. 'It's all lies about a man-of-war,' they said. 'They did not punish the Erromangans. They are afraid of us. Come on, let us kill them!'

Finally, just as one of the warriors swung his tomahawk at John's head, and surrounded by men aiming loaded guns at him, John produced a revolver and pointed it at his attackers. The gun had been given to him by his friend Joseph Copeland, who had insisted he should have a weapon in the house for his own protection. John had no intention of ever shooting any-one, but, as Joseph had foreseen, when the islanders saw he had a gun they took fright. One of the men shouted, 'Missi has got a short musket! He will shoot you all!' When they heard those words the warriors threw themselves flat on the ground in terror.

After a while, the men carefully rose to their feet and ran off into the bush, where they continued yelling and waving their muskets about. Later that night they all left, carrying away with them all the goods they had looted from Abraham's house and the mission store.

When all was quiet, John went to find the local chiefs, Miaki and Nouka. Miaki was very scornful of the missionaries and their God. 'Missi, where was Jehovah today?' he mocked. 'There was no Jehovah today to protect you. It's all lies about Jehovah. They will come and kill you, and Abraham, and his wife, and cut your bodies into pieces to be cooked and eaten in every village upon Tanna.'

But John pointed out, 'Surely, when you had planned all this, and brought them to kill us and steal our property, Jehovah did protect us, or we would not have been here!'

Miaki, however, continued to boast: 'There is no Jehovah today! We have no fear of any man-of-war. They dare not punish us... They will talk to us and say we must not do so again, and give us a present. That is all. We fear nothing. The talk of all Tanna is that we will kill you and seize all your property tomorrow.'

John sent Abraham to Nowar to ask for his advice. The old chief sent back a canoe and a message saying that if John and his helpers came to his house at night with some of their belongings his men would try to protect them.

When the morning came, John heard a conch being sounded close by. Looking out to see what was happening, he saw that it was the signal for a crowd of armed warriors to come running down the hill on the far side of the bay, heading straight for the mission house.

There was not a moment to lose! To stay would mean certain death for John and all those with him. John had stayed on as long as any hope remained of being able to carry on the work. Despite his strongly held belief, based on Scripture, that God was in control of everything, including the time for him to die, he did not believe that meant needlessly throwing away his life, or the lives of his helpers. So he called together Abraham and his wife and Matthew, a teacher who had recently come over from the Mathiesons' mission station to help him, locked the doors and together they quickly set off for Nowar's house.

They had no time to take any of their belongings and had to leave with only the clothes they were wearing. John took his Bible and copies of the Scripture portions he had been able to translate into the Tannese language as well as a couple of lightweight blankets. His faithful dog Clutha went along with them.

He was very sorry at having to leave behind all his dead wife's belongings, including her piano, silver, cutlery and books. He was also forced to leave behind the box containing all his medicines, the clothes sent for distribution to the natives, as well as his own books and other possessions. He later heard that all his property had been sold to traders in exchange for tobacco and weapons and that the men even melted down the lead type from his printing-press to make bullets.

When John and his companions reached Nowar's village they found everyone in a state of panic. The warriors who had come to kill John and his companions had found his house empty and the missionaries gone, so they had decided to pursue them. A large crowd of armed warriors could now be seen approaching. Mothers snatched up their children and ran with them to hide in the bush. Others, filled with terror, waded as far out to sea as they could.

Chief Nowar, who could not go far because of his wounded knee, sat down on an upturned canoe, from where he could watch the enemy approaching. He called John to join him: 'Missi, sit down beside me, and pray to our Jehovah God, for if he does not send deliverance now, we are all dead men. They will kill us all on your account, and that quickly. Pray, and I will watch!'

As Nowar watched, he saw the approaching army come to a halt about three hundred metres away at the foot of the hill leading to the village. He touched John's knee to draw his attention and said softly, 'Missi, Jehovah is hearing! They are all standing still.' All the warriors were standing motionless in complete silence. A man came running along the ranks, giving them some message as he passed. Then the warriors turned round and began to march back the way they had come.

Nowar and his people cried out in great excitement, 'Jehovah has heard Missi's prayer! Jehovah has protected us and turned them away back.' John said afterwards, 'I know not why they turned back; but I have no doubt it was the doing of

God to save our lives.' He joined the others in giving praise and thanks to God for delivering them yet again from what had seemed to be certain death.

After a couple of days Nowar urged John and his companions to leave, because the other tribes were threatening to kill him and his people for sheltering the missionaries. They decided to try to escape to the Mathiesons' mission station. Travel overland was impossible due to the fierce fighting that was going on, but Nowar thought it should be possible by sea. However, John's mission boat and canoe had both been stolen and Miaki had threatened to shoot anyone who tried to use either of them.

There was no hope of escape before nightfall, and as Nowar refused to let him stay in the house a moment longer, John was told to climb up into the branches of a large chestnut tree and hide there until someone came to fetch him. All around him he could hear the sound of gunfire and the yells of the natives, but in the midst of it all he had a wonderful sense of peace and of the Lord's presence with him. As he prayed, telling the Lord everything that was in his heart, he felt that the Lord was speaking to him, comforting him and giving him a real sense of security. Though he was alone, yet in a very real sense he was not alone, because the Lord was with him. He knew that, whatever happened, the Lord would never let him down, not even when the time came for him to die.

About midnight Nowar's son came and called John to climb down out of the tree and follow him down to the shore, where he would find a canoe waiting. However, when they arrived there the owner of the canoe, who had already been paid for its hire, demanded an axe, a sail and a pair of blankets as further payment before he would let them have the canoe. So John had to part with the two blankets which were among the very few things he had been able to rescue from his house. Even then the owner demanded extra payment before he would let them have the paddles, without which the canoe was useless. More than once John offered to call off the whole deal and set off to walk overland to the Mathiesons' house instead. Eventually Nowar and other friends from the village found them three paddles and John, Abraham and his wife and Matthew set off in the frail canoe with a native boy to navigate.

For the first mile or so all went well, but when they rounded a headland they were out on the open sea where they met the full force of the wind and waves head on. The waves threatened to swamp the canoe at any moment and even faithful old Abraham gave up trying to paddle saying, 'Missi, we are all drowned now! We are food for the sharks. We might as well be eaten by the Tannese as by fishes; but God will give us life with Jesus in heaven!'

John, however, was not going to give up. Seizing one of the paddles, he ordered Abraham to grab one of the others and Matthew to start baling the seawater out of the canoe for all he was worth. 'Abraham, where is now your faith in Jesus?' he challenged his old friend. 'Remember, he is ruler on sea as on land. Abraham, pray and ply your paddle! Keep up stroke for stroke with me, as our lives depend on it. Our God can protect us. Matthew, bail with all your might. Don't look round on the sea and fear. Let us pray to God and ply our paddles, and he will save us yet!'

Taking hold of his paddle again, Abraham admitted he had been wrong: 'Thank you for that, Missi. I will be strong. I pray to God and ply my paddle. God will save us!'

Very slowly and with a great deal of effort, they managed to turn the canoe round and paddle their way back towards the shore, eventually landing at the very spot which they had left five hours earlier. They were all soaked to the skin and the men's hands were raw, where the skin had stuck to the paddles.

As soon as they waded ashore, the native lad ran off into the bush, but John was so exhausted that he lay down on the beach and immediately fell fast asleep. Some time later he was woken when he felt someone trying to steal the bag which he was using as a pillow, and which contained his Bible and the passages of Scripture he had translated into the Tannese language. Grabbing hold of the bag, John jumped to his feet and the thief quickly ran off.

John, Abraham and his wife and Matthew knelt together on the sand to thank the Lord for rescuing them from the sea and to ask his help as to what to do next. They fully expected that they might die at any moment.

To think about

John's courage was great in the difficult circumstances he faced. We might wonder how we will cope when the going gets tough.

We must be like John, whose faith in God was strong. He was well aware of the promises of God that he would never desert his people, not in life nor in death. He knew such passages of Scriptures as: 'For he himself has said, "I will never leave you nor forsake you." So we may boldly say: "The Lord is my helper; I will not fear. What can man do to me?"' (Hebrews 13:5-6).

When you face problems and difficulties read Romans 8:28-39. These words echo what Christ said of his people — that no one is able to pluck them out of his hands (John 10:28-30).

John was weak, but his God was strong. John's God is the same God worshipped by all true Christians. We all need to trust him in the same way as John did. Have you learned to trust him like that?

15.
Farewell to Tanna

While John and his friends were sitting on the shore consider-
ing what to do next, Nowar's son-in-law Faimungo suddenly
appeared to warn them that they were in great danger because
Miaki and his men were not far off and were planning to attack
them. Faimungo's home lay in the direction the missionaries
wanted to go, so John asked him to let them follow him and
show them the path.

Faimungo was alarmed at this suggestion. 'Missi, you will
be killed,' he said. 'I dare not let you follow. I have only about
twenty men, and your following might put us all in danger.'

However, John insisted that they were not asking him to
protect them, but just to let them follow at a distance. Eventually, Faimungo said he would just take the seven men who
were with him. He told John, 'I will go, but if you follow you
will be killed on the way. You may follow me as far as you
can!' When they were ready to leave, he and his men ducked
under the shelter of a clump of coconut palms to keep out of
sight. As they ran off they called out, 'Be quick! Follow and
keep as near to us as you can.'

John and his friends set off after them through the bush. At
first the only people they met were friendly, but after about
four miles travelling along the pathway they met a large party
of Miaki's men. The warriors surrounded John and threatened

to shoot him, but Faimungo waved his spear and told them, 'No, you shall not kill Missi today. He is with me.' With those words he strode off into the bush after his men, followed by Abraham, Matthew and Abraham's wife, leaving John alone in the middle of a circle of warriors who all aimed their muskets at him.

As the others all disappeared into the bush Sirawia, who was in command of the party surrounding John, called out after Faimungo, 'Your conduct is bad in taking Missi away. Leave him to us to be killed!'

Sirawia had once been friendly to the missionaries, and John reminded him of those days by saying, 'Sirawia, I love you all. You must know that I sought only your good. I gave you medicine and food when you and your people were sick and dying under measles; I gave you the very clothing you wear. Am I not your friend? Have we not often drunk tea and eaten together in my house? Can you stand there and see your friend shot? If you do, my God will punish you severely.'

Sirawia then whispered something to his men which John could not hear. Seeing that they were not about to fire, John began edging slowly away from them, walking backwards so that he could keep his eyes fixed on them until he was in among the trees out of their sight. Then he turned round and ran after his friends as fast as he could. The warriors did not follow him. Once again God had shown his wonderful power in preserving John's life.

When they came to a village near Faimungo's home, the chief decided it was safe to sit down and take a short rest. The sun was very hot and they were all very weary by now. However, they had only stopped for a few minutes when they heard shouts and the tramp of marching feet. It was another party of hostile warriors approaching.

As the tribesmen came pouring into the open space in the centre of the village, Faimungo told John and his three companions to go on ahead, saying, 'I will follow when I have had a smoke and a talk with these men.'

But John knew that for them to go on by themselves would mean almost certain death. He told Faimungo, 'No, I will stand by your side till you go, and if I am killed, it will be by your side. I will not leave you.'

One of the warriors threw one of the stones which they used to kill people, but it simply grazed Abraham's cheek. Abraham caught John's eye and glanced up to heaven as if to say, 'Missi, I was nearly away to Jesus.' Then there followed a blow from a club which also missed its aim.

The warriors formed a circle round John and his friends, urging each other to strike the first blow or fire the first shot. At that moment John felt an overwhelming sense of assurance that the Lord Jesus was watching the whole scene: 'My peace came back to me like a wave from God,' he said afterwards. 'I realized that I was immortal till my Master's work with me was done. The assurance came to me, as if a voice out of heaven had spoken, that not a musket would be fired to wound us, not a club prevail to strike us, not a spear leave the hand in which it was held vibrating to be thrown, not an arrow leave the bow, or a killing stone the fingers, without the permission of Jesus Christ, whose is all power in heaven and on earth. He rules all nature ... and restrains even the savage of the South Seas.'

John was only human and he knew what it was to experience very real fear in the face of death, so that his whole body was shaking and he could hardly see, but at the same time he was always reminded of the Lord's promise: 'Lo, I am with you always.' Even in such times of crisis he could truly say with the apostle Paul, 'I am persuaded that neither death nor life ... nor any other created thing, shall be able to separate us from the love of God which is in Christ Jesus our Lord.'

Eventually Faimungo agreed to go on and lead the way, telling John, 'Missi, keep close to me.' As they set off, the

warriors ran along on both sides of the path they were following, but they did not attack. At one point, where they had to
cross a stream, John became separated from the others when
he failed to clear the stream in a single leap and fell on his
hands and knees. At that moment he heard a crash in the
branches overhead and realized someone had thrown one of
the killing stones at him, but it had hit a branch of the tree
instead. He scrambled up the bank and followed the track
taken by Faimungo and his friends. When they came to the
stream the warriors who had been pursuing him stopped and
decided to turn back. Once again John praised God for keeping
him safe and restraining the men from attacking.

In the next few villages they came to, all the people knew
Faimungo as one of the most powerful chiefs in that part of the
island. John knew that they would not shoot at him if he kept
close to the chief, for fear of hitting the wrong man.

One group of men whom they met said that Miaki and
others had told them they should kill John because he had
brought the sickness and the hurricanes.

Faimungo told them, 'They lie about Missi! It is our own
bad conduct that makes us sick.'

When they still went on talking about killing foreigners,
Faimungo placed himself between them and John and threatened them with his club and spear. 'You won't kill Missi
today!' he told them.

All the party were very weary from walking for hours in the
hot sun. They were parched with thirst, but did not dare to stop
even for a moment, or bend down to drink at one of the many
streams they crossed, because had they done so, they would
almost certainly have been killed. At last, as they were
approaching the boundary of Faimungo's lands on the far side,
the chief sat down, saying, 'Missi, I have now fulfilled my
promise. I am so tired, I am so afraid, I dare not go further.'

He sent three of his men on with John and his friends to show them the path as far as the next clump of rocks. However, when they had only gone a little way the men told John, 'We dare not go! Faimungo is at war with the people of the next land.' With the simple instruction, 'You must keep straight along this path,' they turned back and ran home to their own village, leaving John and his three companions to go on by themselves.

When they passed one village where they expected trouble because the natives were very hostile, they met only three young lads. All the women and children ran away in terror as they approached. The warriors were all away fighting somewhere else!

Then they were chased by two young men armed with spears. John pulled his revolver out of the bag he was carrying and, pointing it at them, said, 'Beware! Lay down your spears at once on the sand, and carry my basket to the next landing at the Black Rocks.' The young men did as they were told and ran on ahead as far as the rocks, which marked the boundary with the next tribe's land. Putting down John's bag, they begged him, 'Missi, let us return to our home!' Then they ran off as fast as they could.

At last John and his companions came in sight of the mission house, where Mr and Mrs Mathieson came running out to meet them. They had heard that John and the others had left the mission station on the other side of the island and they were relieved to see them alive and well. But they themselves were both in very poor health and were very sad because their only child had recently died.

Before setting off for the Mathiesons', John had left behind with Chief Nowar several letters for the captains of any ships that might call in at the harbour. These letters explained the danger the missionaries were in and asked if the ships would call at the Mathiesons' mission station to rescue them. Each day the missionaries watched hopefully for a ship to appear, but several days passed with no sign of any vessel. When at last a ship was seen out at sea it sailed away without calling for them, even though John hoisted a flag to attract the captain's attention.

Meanwhile they continued to hold public worship services at the Mathiesons' home and on the first Lord's Day after John arrived they also visited some of the nearby villages to hold services. As they were leaving one of the villages a man armed with a club insisted on accompanying them. At one place where the path forked John had to go in front of him. As he did so the man raised his club in the air to strike John over the head. Mr Mathieson, who was walking just behind, shouted out to warn John and leapt forward to grab the club from behind. Hearing the shout, John quickly turned round and between them the two missionaries were able to wrench the club out of the warrior's hands. They made him walk in front of them till they reached the next village, where they would be safe. When they handed back his club he hurried quickly away into the bush.

In the villages they were told that ships had called at the harbour back at John's old home and Miaki had sold all John's clothes and his other belongings to the traders in exchange for guns and ammunition. They also heard from the local people that Miaki's men were going around among the natives who lived near the Mathiesons' home, encouraging them to kill the missionaries.

One day a group of Miaki's men arrived at the house, and forced Mrs Mathieson to show them around. John was busy writing in a small room which led off one of the larger rooms and had locked the door. Although the men went through all the main rooms, they did not notice the door into the little room where John was working and so they did not see him. Before they left they fired a shot into the teachers' house but no one was hurt.

That night John was woken by his faithful dog Clutha, who jumped on him and tugged at the bedclothes until he got up to see what was happening. Realizing that there was someone lurking outside, John woke the Mathiesons, being careful not to make a noise. Peering carefully out into the darkness, they saw that the house was completely surrounded by armed natives. As they watched they saw men walking about carrying burning torches. The men set fire to the church building and then to a fence which ran between the church and the house.

John realized that in a few minutes the house would catch fire and the natives would be waiting outside to kill them all the moment they tried to escape. Taking his revolver in one hand and a tomahawk in the other, he begged Mr Mathieson to quickly let him out of the door and lock it again behind him. Mr Mathieson tried to stop him, but eventually agreed since it was their only hope of saving their lives. He and his wife watched anxiously from inside the house and prayed to God to protect John as he ran straight to the blazing fence, tore it down and hurled it away from the house where it would not set fire to the building.

At that moment John was aware of shadows closing in on him and heard someone shout, 'Kill him! Kill him!' He saw seven or eight men standing round him in a circle, all with clubs poised ready to strike. One of the men tried to grab hold of John, but he managed to jump out of the way and, pulling out his revolver as if he meant to shoot, he challenged them: 'Dare to strike me, and my Jehovah God will punish you. He protects us, and will punish you for burning his church, for hatred to his worship and people, and for all your bad conduct. We love you all; and for doing you good only you want to kill us. But our God is here now to protect us and to punish you.'

Just then they all heard a roaring sound, like that of a powerful engine, rushing towards them. As the tornado struck, the strong wind swept the flames right away from the house. Then from the clouds above floods of torrential rain began to fall. Within a few minutes the thatched roof of the house and all the surrounding area were all soaking wet. There was no longer any question of anyone being able to set fire to the building.

For a few moments the warriors were stunned into silence. Then someone shouted, 'That is Jehovah's rain! Truly their Jehovah God is fighting for them and helping them. Let us away!' With that they dropped their flaming torches and ran off in a panic.

When they had all gone John went back to the house door and called out, 'Open and let me in. I am now all alone.'

Mr Mathieson opened the door to let him, saying as he did so, 'If ever, in time of need, God sent help and protection to his servants in answer to prayer, he has done so tonight!' The three of them joined in praising God, who had sent the storm at just the right moment, and in just the right direction to blow the flames away from the house, instead of towards it.

John lay awake the rest of the night listening, and Clutha kept watch at his side with her ears pricked, but all was quiet till the morning. Then some of the local people came to tell them a crowd of warriors were on their way to kill the missionaries and loot and burn their house.

They could hear the warriors yelling as they approached. At the same time the villagers were all crying and wondering if they should run for their lives. But suddenly, over all the noise and excitement, the cry went up: 'Sail O! Sail O!' For a moment the missionaries thought they were imagining it, but then the villagers all took up the shout one after the other and a few minutes later they could see for themselves a ship approaching. It was one of the trading ships, called the *Blue*

Bell, and its crew were among those who had bought John's clothes and other stolen property from Miaki and his men.

John hurried to the nearby hillside where he set fire to the reeds in order to make a lot of smoke and so attract the attention of the men on the ship. Then he quickly went back to the house and tied a white sheet to one end of the building and a black shawl to the other.

The captain, who had, as it turned out, been asked by John's friends on Aneityum to call and see if the missionaries were all right, sent two boats to the shore with a party of twenty armed men, under the command of the mate. One of the boats soon returned to the ship with the first boatload of the Mathiesons' belongings, while some of the men from the ship remained behind and helped the missionaries pack the rest of the things they wanted to take and carry them down to the beach ready to be ferried out to the *Blue Bell.*

By two o'clock in the afternoon both boats were fully loaded and the missionaries were ready to leave. Suddenly, however, Mr Mathieson, who was terribly upset at having to leave, locked himself in his study and refused to come out, telling John and Mrs Mathieson to leave without him. He said he was going to stay behind on Tanna and die as a martyr.

John pleaded with him to come out and Mrs Mathieson was in tears as she tried to persuade her husband to come with them. This went on for several hours until it was nearly dark.

Finally, John shouted to Mr Mathieson through the locked door, 'It is now getting dark. Your wife must go with the vessel, but I will not leave you alone. I shall send a note explaining why I am forced to remain; and as it is certain that we shall be murdered whenever the vessel leaves, I tell you God will charge you with the guilt of our murder.'

At last Mr Mathieson unlocked the door and came out. They all made their way to the beach and the two waiting boats. However, because of the long wait and the changing tides, the

Blue Bell was no longer in sight by the time the boats put out to sea. For some hours they drifted in the darkness and eventually, after asking the advice of John and his companions, the sailors decided to make for the harbour at Port Resolution, close to John's old mission station, where they could wait for the ship. They found their way by the glow coming from the volcano on the island, which could be seen miles out at sea.

When they came in sight of the harbour they anchored well out of range of musket shots from the shore and sat waiting for the ship. Hours passed and still there was no sign of the *Blue Bell*. Eventually the mate decided to take one of the boats and set off to find the ship, leaving the passengers and some of the less able seamen in the boat still anchored off the shore.

During the afternoon, after the other boat had left, a canoe approached from the shore with the chiefs Nowar and Miaki on board. Miaki tried to persuade John to go back to the mission house, claiming that he would find everything still as he had left it. However, John knew this was not true because Abraham and a few others had already tried to go ashore in a canoe and had found armed men surrounding the house. All the windows had been smashed and John's things were all gone. In fact John had seen sailors from the *Blue Bell* wearing some of his clothes which they had bought from the natives!

When Miaki saw that his plan to lure the missionaries back on land had failed he admitted, 'We have taken everything your house contained, and would take you too if we could, for we hate the worship. It causes all our diseases and deaths; it goes against our customs, and it condemns the things we delight in.'

When Nowar heard that all the people in the boat had been without food since the morning of the previous day he brought them some coconuts, and roasted yams for Mrs Mathieson and Abraham's wife. However, with the hot sun beating down on

Sketch of volcano on Tanna by Margaret Paton

the open boat, they were all parched with thirst and trying to eat the food only made this worse.

At last, at about five o'clock in the evening, the *Blue Bell* came into view and by nightfall the passengers, with all the goods they had been able to bring with them in the two boats, were safely on board. They all arrived safely in Aneityum and the ship's captain refused to take any money from them for the fare. Instead the missionaries decided to share out the fare money among the sailors, who had been very kind to them on the voyage.

Sadly, within a few weeks of their arrival Mrs Mathieson became seriously ill with a lung disease and soon afterwards died. A few months later her husband also went to be with their Lord and Saviour, Jesus Christ, leaving John as the only surviving missionary who had worked on any of the northern islands in the New Hebrides.

John's original idea was that he would remain on the island of Aneityum and continue with the translation of the Scriptures into Tannese, hoping that one day God would open up the way for him to return to Tanna to take up the work there again.

However, the other missionaries, including his friend Joseph Copeland, persuaded him to take the opportunity of sailing to Australia on a ship that was leaving in a few days' time. They wanted him to visit the churches, telling them about the urgent need for missionaries in the New Hebrides and trying to arouse their interest in the work there. Up till now all the missionaries had come from Scotland or Canada and little was known about the work in Australia or New Zealand. As well as recruiting new workers they also needed to raise money so they could buy another ship for the mission.

To think about

John spent much time in prayer and worship, even in the most difficult situations. Martin Luther spent four hours each day with God in prayer and meditation upon his Word. For some reason most Christians believe they can face a hostile world without spending much time with the Lord. Why is this so?

I think we have things so easy in our Western world that we see little need of God's help; we believe we can do things in our own strength. If only we realized that great things could be accomplished in the strength of our God, then great things would be accomplished. We are weak beings and will only achieve small things when acting in our own strength. Let us develop a sound prayer life and set aside a time each day for communion with God.

We also find that an exhausted John was told to leave for Australia. He needed a rest. We all need times of rest and relaxation in the midst of our busy lives in order to gain new strength to carry out God's work.

16.
Taking the message to Australia

For the sum of £10 John secured a passage on a sandalwood trading-ship which was ready to set sail for Sydney. Once on board, his first job was to make a new shirt for himself. He had escaped from Tanna with only the clothes on his back. All the rest had been stolen by the natives and even when he saw some of the sailors on the *Blue Bell* wearing his shirts, which they had bought off the islanders, they would not let him have any of them back.

The captain of the sandalwood trader was a cruel, godless man, who was constantly fighting with his crew and generally making everyone's life on board thoroughly miserable. There were a number of islanders on board who did not know a word of English, and no one on the ship could speak their language, but the crew forced them to work by pushing and pulling them about and hitting them until they did what they were supposed to do. When they arrived in Sydney these men would be sold for slave labour on the Queensland sugar plantations.

As the only cabin on board was occupied by the ship's captain and his native wife, John was given a place to sleep in the part of the hold where the sandalwood was stored. He was forced to sleep on bare boards for the whole of the 1,400-mile journey and there was nowhere he could take his clothes off to wash. Except when it was raining he spent the whole day up on the open deck. His food, which was sent up to him there, was scarcely fit for a dog to eat. He could hardly wait to get off the ship when it arrived in Sydney harbour.

John had not been given any formal papers by the mission which he could show to the churches in Australia explaining the purpose of his visit, or the work he had been authorized to carry out. All he carried was a letter of introduction to one man. When John went to see this man, he agreed to introduce John to various ministers, but though they were all very polite, John found that they always had some excuse why they could not ask him to speak in their churches. It was only later that he discovered the reason for this. It turned out that the man to whom the letter of introduction was addressed had recently published a series of newspaper articles which were causing a lot of trouble among the local churches. So all the ministers were wary of inviting anyone recommended by him!

John prayed to the Lord for guidance and soon met a kindly Christian couple, Mr and Mrs Foss, who invited him to lodge in their home while he was in Sydney. They told him they could introduce him to a number of Christians who would be able to help him in his work.

On his second Sunday in the town, he went out in the afternoon and noticed a lot of children going into the Chalmers Presbyterian Church for the Sunday School. Believing God was guiding him, he went in and spoke to the minister, who agreed to let him speak to the children for a few minutes about the mission. He then invited John to address the congregation at the evening service.

The next day the minister introduced John to several other local pastors and within a very short time invitations to speak began to pour in from all over the area. John formed a committee of local ministers, whom people knew and respected, to take charge of all the money raised for the work of the mission.

He also thought of a wonderful scheme to involve the Sunday School children in the building of the mission ship. He had share certificates printed, each with a value of sixpence. As each child gave sixpence to the work of the mission he or she received a share certificate stating that the child was one of the shareholders in the ship. In other words, between them, they owned the ship: it was their very own ship! In this way John established what he was to describe as a 'shipping company for Jesus'. Thousands of these share certificates were issued, as more and more families contributed. Many of the children who bought them went on supporting the work of the mission when they were grown up and in time taught their own children to save their pennies to buy shares in the mission ships.

Soon John was travelling all over south-eastern Australia and so much money was coming in that the mission were able to start building a bigger ship than the one they had originally planned. Money was also set aside for supporting more native teachers like John's old friend Abraham. Often a Sunday School, or sometimes even an individual person, would undertake the sponsorship of their own native teacher, promising to give enough money each year to pay for the teacher's salary. This, of course, gave them a special interest in the work of the teacher they supported.

Wherever he went, John used to take with him a bag containing various articles of native dress, clubs, arrows and even some of the idols used in worship by the islanders of the New Hebrides. He used these to illustrate his talks and help people to imagine what life was really like on Tanna and the other islands.

As he travelled around, John was constantly aware of the hand of God guiding his every step. Many of his journeys took him through the Australian outback, where there were no proper roads, just dusty tracks across the open country where the traveller found his way by following notches which had been cut in tree-trunks by the roadside. If someone lost his way he had to retrace his footsteps to the last notch he had seen and have another try at working out which way he was meant to go!

Once John was given a lift along some of these tracks in a horse-drawn buggy by a driver who told him, 'I know this road well.'

The two men were soon deep in conversation and it was about three hours later that John suddenly said to the driver, 'Surely we cannot have turned back! Those trees and bushes are wonderfully like those we passed at starting!'

The man laughed and said, 'I am too old a hand in the bush for that! I have gone this road many a time before.'

However, a few minutes later they saw an inn which John was sure he recognized as the one from which they had started out three hours earlier. They stopped a man whom they saw coming along the road to ask for directions, and discovered that they had indeed come back to their starting-point!

In winter the roads were often not passable for vehicles and John sometimes had to walk miles on foot, carrying his heavy bag. One dark night he lost the path and found he was sinking deeper in the mud of a swamp with every step he took, so he just had to stand still and wait for someone to come by. He kept praying to the Lord to help him. At last at about midnight he heard voices and began calling out until the men heard him and came to help him. The farmer who pulled him out of the swamp said that if they had not found him he would have been dead by the morning.

Once when John was travelling by coach he found he was sitting next to a fellow Scotsman. The man noticed John was reading a book as he travelled and after a while he asked, 'Are you a minister?'

'Yes,' John replied.

'Where is your church?' the man wanted to know.

'I have no church.'

The questions and answers went on like a catechism:

'Where is your home?'

'I have no home.'

'Where have you come from?'

'The South Sea Islands.'

'What are you doing in Australia?'

'Pleading the cause of the mission.'

'Are you a Presbyterian?'

'I am.'

The man was so impressed by what John told him about the mission that he insisted on paying the missionary's coach-fare, saying that to do so was 'a joy to me, sir, a great joy; I honour you for your work's sake!'

On another occasion John stopped at an isolated cattle station where the owner was a rough Irishman. When he explained who he was and asked if he could stop for a rest before continuing his journey, the man shouted at him to be off: 'Go on! I don't want to be troubled with the likes of you here!'

John quietly answered, 'I am sorry if my coming troubles you, but I wish you every blessing in Christ Jesus. Goodbye!' and prepared to drive off. However, at that moment a lady called out from the house, 'Don't let that missionary go away!' She had heard John speak in Melbourne and wanted to see the things he carried in his bag. So John was called back and spent a quarter of an hour explaining about the work of the mission. As he left, the rough farmer who had shouted at John to go away pressed a cheque for £5 into his hands and wished him great success in his work.

One Saturday John faced a journey of twenty-two miles to the place where he was to hold a meeting and stop overnight. There was no transport available, so a young lady offered him the loan of her racehorse, called Garibaldi, saying that if he left the horse at the end of the journey, she would collect him later. As the horse could not carry John's luggage, arrangements were made for a friend to bring it on afterwards.

John was not very expert at horse-riding, but as there was no other way of reaching his destination, he set off, clinging on tightly and making the horse walk at a very sedate pace. After a little while they were overtaken by three men on horseback who laughed at the awkward way John was sitting in the saddle. The next moment Garibaldi, who seemed to think it was beneath his honour as a racehorse to let himself be overtaken in this way, laid back his ears, stretched out his neck and launched into a gallop. He flew past the three other riders like the wind, with John desperately hanging onto the bridle, and dashed past all the notches on the trees so fast that John did not have a hope of seeing any of them, but the horse seemed to know where he was going.

To make matters worse, a thunderstorm broke around them and every time the lightning flashed and the thunder roared Garibaldi ran even faster. John's clothes were drenched from the rain and spattered with mud flying from the horse's hooves. He was wearing a hat with a high crown and this was all battered and out of shape as he rammed it hard down over his head to stop it getting knocked off by an overhanging tree-branch.

As they raced helter-skelter towards the house where John was to stay overnight, people were watching from the windows for the missionary to arrive. They all rushed to the verandah when they saw the mud-spattered figure clinging on to the back of the runaway house as it came pounding in through the gateway. A young groom from the stables threw the gate open just in time and hung on to the horse's bridle until he finally brought it to a halt just outside the door.

John was so shaken by his experience that when he was helped down from the horse he could not stand upright and promptly sat down in the mud. When he tried to speak, the words would not come out properly! He had great trouble convincing the people of the house that he was not drunk — in fact he was a teetotaller and never touched alcohol.

Then the farmer suggested he change his clothes, which were dripping wet and covered in mud. John had to explain: 'Yes, but my bag is coming on the cart, and may not be here tonight.' The farmer lent him a change of clothes, but they were much too big for John and only made him look even more ridiculous. When he joined the company for tea and tried to explain what had happened everyone burst out laughing.

Eventually John was able to speak at the meeting as planned and his talks there and at the church the next day were well received, but he never forgot that ride. Nor did the farmer's wife, who often amused her friends afterwards with the tale of her first meeting with the famous missionary.

It was when John was waiting for someone to come and fetch him after the coach service had broken down on one of his journeys on the bad cross-country roads that he first came into contact with some of the Australian Aborigines. A large number of them, who had gathered for a sports day, spent the whole of the Sunday morning fighting each other and rushing around the open space in front of the church, yelling so loudly that they disrupted the service.

In the afternoon John went and spoke to them, making himself understood in broken English and by using sign language. He persuaded them to sit down and, while the women boiled water for tea and baked their rough native bread over campfires, he talked to them about the Lord Jesus. The Aborigines were not used to being shown kindness by white people and after that if a dog chased John, or even barked at him, the women would drive it away with sticks and stones.

John was horrified at the cruel way many people treated the Aborigines, especially the traders who sold them alcohol in exchange for blankets. When the natives became rowdy and violent under the influence of the drink the white people would make their bad behaviour an excuse for killing them and driving them off the land so they could take it over, even though they were the ones who had given them the drink in the first place.

When white people took boys and girls from Aborigine families into their homes to train them as servants or workers they never treated them as equals, and made little effort to teach them about the Lord Jesus or how to worship God. Instead they were treated little better than slaves. Then the white people were surprised if they ran off back to their own people as soon as they were old enough!

Many people actually believed there was no point in teaching the Aborigines the gospel as they considered them to be no better than animals without souls to be saved. But John knew this was not true. In fact he soon discovered, when he met some of them, that they had their own primitive forms of worship which were very much like those of the islanders of the New Hebrides. Before he left Australia he urged the churches to make greater efforts to take the gospel of the Lord Jesus to the Aborigines and teach them about the true God instead of the idols they worshipped.

When John heard of the terrible cruelties meted out to the Aborigines by some of the white settlers, it made him very angry. Speaking of some of these people who had suffered so much, he wrote, 'And their sin, their crime? Oh, only seizing a sheep, in the frenzy of hunger, which fattened on the lands where once grew their food, and from which the white man had pitilessly hunted them!'

John tells the story of an aboriginal Christian lady named Nora Hood whom he met. He was introduced to her by a friend, Roderick Urquhart, who described how he had found Nora living in a camp for black people, in conditions of extreme poverty. When Mr Urquhart and his friends first saw her there she was lying on the floor of the hut, ill. However, she was reading a Bible to several of her friends and explaining to them about the love of the Lord Jesus who died to save lost sinners.

When Mr Urquhart, who knew that Nora had once lived in a more comfortable home until her husband lost his job through drink, said how sorry he was to see her ill and living in such dreadful conditions, she replied, 'The change has indeed made me unwell, but I am beginning to think that this too is for the best; it has at last brought my poor husband to his senses, and I will grudge nothing if God thereby brings him to the Saviour's feet!'

She went on to tell them of the joy it had brought her to tell her own people about the true God and his Son Jesus. Then she added, 'Do not think that I like this miserable hut, or the food, or the company; but I am and have been happy in trying to do good amongst my people.'

When John and another minister visited her hut they found her reading a Christian magazine, *The Presbyterian Messenger*. She told them she read it because she liked to know what was going on in the church. As she sat talking to them they also noticed her well-used Bible lying close to her elbow.

John told her he would like to ask some questions about her people. He began by saying, 'Nora, they tell me you are a Christian... I hope that as a Christian you will speak the truth.'

Nora was rather hurt that John should doubt her word. 'I am a Christian,' she replied. 'I fear and serve the true God. I always speak the truth.'

Later on she corresponded with John. In one of her letters she wrote, 'I am always reading my Bible, for I believe in God the Father and in Christ Jesus our Lord... I always teach my children to pray to God our Father in heaven... Sir, I shall always pray for you, that God may bless and guide you. O, Sir, pray for me, my husband, and my children!'

In another letter she said, I hope you will go home to England safely, get more missionaries, and then go back to your poor blacks on the islands...'

By now enough money had been raised through John's meetings for work to begin on building a ship for the mission. It was to be called the *Dayspring*, and was to be built in Nova Scotia, Canada, the home of the earliest missionaries. As there was now also widespread support for the work of the mission among the churches of Australia, the mission committee suggested that John should go back home to Britain for a time to try to stir up interest among the churches there too and if possible to recruit more missionaries for the New Hebrides.

At first John was not at all sure if it was right for him to spend time travelling to Britain and going round the country visiting churches there, instead of returning immediately to the islands to carry on his work. However, one of the ministers, Dr Cairns, encouraged him to go saying, 'Sir, it is of the Lord. The whole enterprise is of God and not of us. Go home and he will give you more missionaries for the islands.'

John's friends and fellow-missionaries on Aneityum, Dr and Mrs Inglis, had themselves just returned from Britain, where they had been arranging for the New Testament to be printed in the language of the island people, and they too urged John to go.

Finally, after a great deal of prayer, John decided to take the unusual step of casting lots, asking the Lord to show him by this means what he should do. The piece of paper he opened after he had prayed read: 'Go home.' So on 16 May 1863 John set sail on a Scottish ship, the *Kosciusko*, bound for London and for the home he had left five years earlier and had thought he would never see again.

To think about

In Australia John found a lot of support for the ship-building project from children attending Sunday School. This was a big task, but always remember that our God is 'the God of the impossible'. How can church members and Sunday School children today play a part in missionary work? How are you involved in the support of missionary outreach? Do you know that by purchasing this book you are supporting the work of Evangelical Press in missionary endeavour?

John used some good ideas to gain the support he needed. We need to think hard about practical ways in which we can encourage prayer and material support for missionary work.

There is also a work to be done in taking the gospel to our neighbours. If you are a Christian, do you think that your neighbour knows that you are? If not, there is a missionary work for you to do here in your own street.

17.
Home to Scotland and back

The voyage on the *Kosciuko* was much more enjoyable than John's last sea-trip. This time the captain was a Christian and was concerned for the welfare of his passengers. John enjoyed fellowship with other Christians on board and he and another minister took turns in leading worship services for the passengers and crew.

However, the journey was not without incident. As they were rounding the Cape of Good Hope there was a violent thunderstorm and the ship was struck by lightning. Under the impact the ship plunged deeply towards the sea-bottom and then bounced back up again. Everyone who was on deck at the time was thrown flat on the deck. Below in the captain's cabin the passengers were flung off their chairs and hurled into passageways. Some were even knocked unconscious. John found his leg caught between the chair on which he had been sitting and the table. He grabbed hold of the table and tried to pull himself up, but his leg was badly bruised and he had to be carried to his cabin. However, no one was seriously hurt and they all soon recovered, though the captain afterwards became ill with a fever.

When all the injured men had received first aid the captain came to see John and asked him to lead them all in public prayer. 'Let us thank the Lord for this most merciful deliverance,' he said. 'The ship is not on fire, and no one is seriously injured!' He also gave John as a souvenir a piece of copper from the bulwarks of the ship, which had been melted and twisted by the lightning.

On 26 August 1863, three months and ten days after leaving Australia, John set foot on English soil. He had never been in London before and in some ways would have liked to look around the city, but as he was anxious to press on with the work he had come to do, he headed straight for the railway station and caught a train home to Scotland that very night. On his arrival the following morning he reported first to the committee of the mission to arrange a date for a meeting, and then caught the next train for Dumfries and his old home at Torthorwald.

Five years had passed since John had last seen his parents and his homecoming was a very emotional one. They must often have wondered if they would ever see each other again on earth and so much had happened in those short years that there was a lot to talk about. It was a joyful family reunion and they were full of praise to God that once again they were together, but they also wept over the death of John's wife and baby son.

A few days later John travelled to Coldstream, in the Border country of Scotland, to visit the parents of Mary, his beloved wife. This dear couple were still grieving over the loss of their daughter and in fact they never fully recovered from the blow. They accepted her death without ever complaining against the Lord, but their lives and their health were never the same afterwards.

Then it was on to Edinburgh for a meeting of the Foreign Missions Committee of the church that had sent John out to work for the Lord in the New Hebrides. He gave them a full report of what he had been doing and told them of his hopes and plans for the future. They agreed that he should travel throughout Scotland visiting all their congregations and Sunday Schools to tell them about the work of the mission. They also invited him to address the students at their Bible College, or Divinity Hall, as it was called.

The Reformed Presbyterian Church in Scotland, of which John was a member, were so impressed with his work that during this visit they conferred on him the highest honour they could give to anyone by appointing him as Moderator of their Supreme Court. They also placed on record their appreciation of what he had done in raising funds during his time in Australia and their thanks for the support of ministers and Sunday Schools, both at home and in Australia, in getting the *Dayspring* project off the ground.

John was soon off on his travels round Scotland, visiting churches and Sunday Schools and telling them about the work in the New Hebrides. Although the people were not rich, they were very generous, giving not only money but boxes of clothing and other gifts for the islanders.

Unfortunately the dates chosen for his trip to the far north of Scotland were in the middle of winter, when the weather was bitterly cold and the roads covered with snow and ice. John had to travel the twenty or so miles from Wick to Thurso by mail coach, and as all the seats inside the coach were already taken he had to sit outside in the freezing weather. As a result of this journey he suffered frostbite in one of his feet. He had to stay in Thurso for a week because of the bad weather and during all that time he had no feeling in the injured foot.

As soon as there was a lull in the weather John boarded a steamer bound for Stromness in the Orkneys, but soon after they set off the storm blew up again with gale-force winds and heavy seas. All passengers were ordered below deck for safety reasons, but as the air down below was thick with the smell of whisky and tobacco and the passengers were all rough and noisy, John begged the captain to let him remain on the deck.

The captain's first reaction was to shout above the noise of the storm, 'I dare not! You'll be washed overboard.' However, seeing the expression on John's face, he changed his mind and told his men to find a tarpaulin which they tied round and over the top of John and then lashed securely to the mast. The gales were so severe and the sea so rough that it became too dangerous to go on and the ship had to wait for some hours in the shelter of a headland until the weather improved.

By the time they finally landed, John's frostbitten foot was so numb and painful that he could hardly walk one step at a time. He managed to hold two meetings, but had to cancel the others he had planned in the highlands and islands and travel south again in order to receive medical treatment. He had to take a complete rest for two months and there was even talk of amputation. Eventually he was referred to a doctor in Liverpool who specialized in a kind of treatment by electric shock. When this also failed to restore any feeling to John's foot the doctor put a plaster cast on the foot, but this was so painful that after only a day John had to ask him to take it off again. As the doctor did so the frostbitten part of his foot came away with the plaster! The doctor then applied a new plaster to the rest of the foot and before long John was able to walk on it again. However, for the rest of his life he used to feel twinges of pain in that foot whenever he did too much walking.

Even though the trouble with his foot meant that John could not hold all the meetings he had planned, his tour of the Scottish churches was very successful in raising support for the *Dayspring*. He used the same system that he had in Australia, issuing share certificates to the Sunday School children who gave money for the fund, so that in a real sense they owned the ship. Four new missionaries also volunteered to go out to the New Hebrides to work. John's preaching tour helped to raise money for their support and travelling expenses.

Margaret Whitecross Paton, John's second wife

John stayed in Scotland for over a year and during that time he met a lady named Margaret Whitecross. She was a fine Christian and very gifted in many ways. She also came from a family who were keenly interested in missionary work. As they got to know each other, she and John became convinced that, both in her education and her family background, the Lord had been preparing her to serve him overseas as John's wife. Some time in 1864 they were married at a service held at her sister's home in Edinburgh.

Soon it was time for the newly married couple to say goodbye to all their family and friends in Scotland. John and Margaret travelled to Torthorwald to take their leave of John's parents. It was a very moving time for all of them, because his parents were by now growing very old and they knew that they were not likely to see one another again until they all met in heaven. They all knelt together in prayer as old James Paton, with his long white hair falling over his shoulders, committed his son and new daughter-in-law to the Lord's keeping. John's mother kept back her tears until he and Margaret had gone, but then she fell fainting into the arms of her younger son and it took a long time for her to come round. However, the family took great comfort in the knowledge that the parting was not for ever and that, as all of them were true believers in Christ, they would all one day be reunited in the Lord's presence.

John and Margaret travelled south to Liverpool and there boarded the *Crest of the Wave*, which set sail for Australia in October 1864. The new missionaries who had volunteered to serve in the islands stayed behind to do some medical training before following on a later ship. During his time on Tanna John had found his own medical training invaluable and he urged all future missionaries to gain a thorough grounding in the basics of medicine before setting out for these remote islands where there were, of course, no other medical facilities.

After a voyage of ninety-five days (which was very fast for those days) John and Margaret landed at Sydney on 17 January 1865. No sooner had their ship docked than John learnt that the new mission ship, the *Dayspring*, had arrived in Sydney harbour. On the way to Australia the ship had called at the New Hebrides, bringing new missionaries from Canada. But now there was trouble because the crew had not been paid and there was no money to pay them their wages, or to cover the day-to-day running expenses of the ship. John paid the captain £50 out

Gravestone in Torthorwald churchyard recording the deaths of John's parents and other members of the Paton family, including John himself even though, as the stone records, he and some of the others named were buried elsewhere (see also picture p.67).

of his own pocket to meet the most urgent demands and asked
for a few days in which to try to raise the rest of the money.

One of the first things he did when he landed was to go and
have a look at the new ship. She was a beautiful, two-masted
sailing-ship — just right for taking the missionaries to and
from the islands and keeping them well supplied with what
they needed. As John stood on the quayside gazing at her, he
thought of all the Sunday School children whose pennies had
gone to pay for her and told himself, 'The Lord has provided
— the Lord will provide.'

The first *Dayspring*

After praying to the Lord and asking him to supply the
money which was so necessary if the missionaries were to
carry on the work to which God had called them, John first
asked his friends for advice, but they were not very helpful.
Then he made enquiries about borrowing money. This created
great problems as, on the one hand, the interest rates were too
high and there would have been a serious risk of losing the ship
if all the money were not found in time; on the other hand,
nothing could be arranged without authority in writing from
Scotland, and there was no time to wait for that.

In desperation John called a meeting of ministers and other friends interested in the mission. He gave them a report of his overseas trip and then explained the problem about money for the *Dayspring*.

Some of those present said, 'Sell her, and have done with it!'

Others said that since the Sunday Schools had given them this ship, the least they could do was to find the money to keep it afloat.

John reminded the meeting that the missionaries gave their whole lives to the work of taking the gospel to the natives, and their salaries of only £120 a year were mainly paid by the churches in Scotland and Canada. Surely it was not too much to ask of the churches in Australia to accept the responsibility for the running costs of the ship which was so essential to the work of the mission?

That Sunday John held services in the local churches at which he told them of the need for money for the ship.

After the morning service in a little mission hall near the harbour, a couple came up to John and explained that the husband was the captain of a ship which had just arrived in port and was now lying at anchor opposite the *Dayspring*. The captain told John, 'My wife and I, being too late to get on shore to attend any church in the city, heard this little chapel bell ringing, and followed, when we saw you going up the hill. We have so enjoyed the service... This cheque for £50 will be a beginning to help you out of your difficulties.'

John knew that God had arranged it that the couple would be too late to go to the church they had planned to attend, in order that they would come to the service where they heard about the need for money for the mission ship.

And this was just the beginning. In the service that afternoon, when John told the congregation what had happened, people began to stand up from their seats and say, 'I will give you £10,' or 'I shall send you £20 tomorrow morning.' Soon the money began to pour in through the post. Once again, God had answered John's prayers and honoured his faith in a wonderful way!

As well as the mission which had sent John out to the New Hebrides, the Lordon Missionary Society had missionaries working in that part of the world and they too owned a ship, the *John Williams*. Some of the churches felt it was too much to expect local Christians to support the work of both missions and both ships, so they suggested that John should travel further afield to other parts of Australia to raise the money for the *Dayspring*. John was very concerned that there should not be any rivalry or competition between the two missions, who were both carrying out important work for the Lord and indeed worked well together on the mission-field.

So once more John set off, this time on board the *Dayspring* itself, on a fund-raising tour round Australia — even visiting the island state of Tasmania. Special trips were arranged and thousands of children came with their parents to see their own special mission ship. Almost every day, and often more than once in the day, John spoke at meetings, telling about the work of the mission and explaining the urgent need of money for the ship. At last, after months of such meetings and many weary miles of travelling, all the money that was needed to pay off the outstanding debt on the *Dayspring* had been raised.

John wanted to avoid once and for all having to spend further time and effort on this type of emergency appeal for money, so he urged the local Presbyterian churches and Sunday Schools to band together to make proper arrangements for the ship's expenses to be met on a regular basis. This would put an end to the need for special appeals and fund-raising tours. At last the church authorities agreed and the *Dayspring* became the special responsibility of the Australian Presbyterian Churches.

In May 1865 John and Margaret finally set sail on the *Dayspring* for the islands of the New Hebrides, with their baby son, Bob, who had been born while they were in Australia.

To think about

John was always thrilled to receive help from his supporters in other countries. If you are a Christian you must be supporting those who take the good news concerning Christ to the people of the world who have not heard the true gospel.

John was also concerned with the education of missionaries. Think about the type of training today's missionaries need and if you have the inclination put your suggestions into the hands of the church committee responsible for training missionaries.

Today it is difficult for preachers of the gospel to gain entry to many countries. Some additional skill is often needed before such people are permitted to enter communities overseas. Doctors, nurses and teachers are usually welcomed with open arms in developing countries where preachers may not readily be admitted.

Maybe younger people reading this book should give some consideration to this matter when making decisions concerning the profession they plan to follow. Ask yourself, 'Is this the best way I can serve the Lord, here or overseas?'

18.
A British warship comes to call

John hoped the time had now come for him to resume his work among the islanders of the New Hebrides, but when he arrived in Aneityum for a meeting with the other missionaries they told him that the best thing he could do to help them would be to return to Australia to make sure the arrangements for the money needed for the support of the *Dayspring* were on a permanent footing. So, after only a short stay, in which they travelled around several of the islands on the *Dayspring,* meeting the local Christian workers, and Margaret had her very first glimpses of the islands where she hoped to make her home, they reluctantly turned round and set sail once more for Australia.

However, in the short time they were in the New Hebrides an incident occurred which was to cause a lot of trouble and unpleasantness for John. A British man-of-war, the H.M.S. *Curaçoa,* arrived at Aneityum under the command of Commodore Sir William Wiseman. The ship had come because some time earlier the mission leaders had sent a petition to the British government asking them to hold an official enquiry into the murder of the missionaries George and Ellen Gordon on the island of Erromanga and the violence which had forced John and the other missionaries to leave Tanna and the island of Efatè.

Since the commodore did not speak any of the local languages, he asked the mission for interpreters and John agreed to act as interpreter when the ship called at Tanna. The man-of-war then sailed to each of the islands in turn where the commodore told the natives, through the interpreters, that he had been sent by Queen Victoria to look into the complaints that had been made and punish those who had done wrong.

'No one is trying to force you to become Christians,' he told them, 'but you encouraged white people to come and live among you, and you sold them land and promised to protect them. But instead of keeping those promises, you killed some of them and tried to kill others, and you stole or destroyed their property.' This had to stop, the captain warned. In future, the queen would send a ship every year to make sure that they were not killing her people and to punish anyone who was guilty. At the same time, if the islanders had suffered at the hands of any of the white men (such as the cruel sandalwood traders) they would have the right to make a complaint to the queen's representatives. Queen Victoria would then see to it that the guilty men were punished.

When the *Curaçoa* reached Tanna, the commodore spent three days talking to the natives, with John acting as interpreter, trying to find out who were the ones responsible for the attacks on the missionaries and for the murder of a white trader. The captain warned the islanders that if they would not co-operate with him and tell him who the ringleaders and murderers were, he would fire his cannon at two villages which belonged to a chief who was known to have killed a white man. He would also destroy the chief's canoes.

However, since Chief Nowar had helped to protect John and his friends when they were in danger, the captain promised that he and his people would be safe. He also said that if the people from the two villages he had threatened to shoot left their homes and took refuge in Nowar's lands they too would not be in any danger, though they would lose their homes. He did not want to kill people, just to make a show of force to frighten the natives so that they would not harm any white men in future.

All the inhabitants of the two villages escaped to Nowar's lands, where they were safe, but as the time set for the ships' guns to be fired drew near, a crowd of angry warriors gathered on the beach, all wearing war-paint and carrying weapons. They announced that they were going to fight the British man-of-war.

Seeing the sailors preparing to open fire, John went up to the commodore and begged him, with tears in his eyes, 'Surely you are not going to shell these poor and foolish Tannese!'

However, the captain was not going to be put off. 'You are here as interpreter, not as my adviser,' he told John. 'If I leave without punishing them now, no vessel or white man will be safe at this harbour. You can go on board your own ship, till I require your services again.'

He then told his men to open fire. The first shell exploded in the bush on a hillside just below the spot where a group of tribesmen were in the middle of a ritual war-dance in defiance of the commodore and his crew. Lumps of earth and bushes were tossed into the air from the force of the explosion, and the next moment all the dancers could be seen rapidly disappearing over the brow of the hill.

Another two shots were fired over the heads of the crowd of warriors gathered on the shore. Amid a great deal of noise and confusion, all the men immediately rushed off in the direction of Nowar's lands.

Then the commodore turned the guns on the two villages, as he had threatened, and blew the houses to pieces. Soon afterwards a party of men were sent ashore in a boat to destroy the remaining houses and canoes. None of the natives was killed and only one man was hurt, though there was a report that three tribesmen were killed later when one of the fallen cannonballs exploded as they were trying to strip it down to use as ammunition in their own guns. One of the sailors who had been sent ashore to destroy the villages was also shot when he wandered away from the rest of his party, against the captain's orders, and the tribesmen found him standing in one of their plantations munching on a stick of sugar-cane.

However, when John stepped ashore in Sydney, ready to take up his campaigning once more on behalf of the mission, he found that everyone was talking about H.M.S. *Curaçoa*'s visit to the islands and blaming him and the other missionaries for helping to kill tribesmen! The newspapers had somehow got hold of a false version of the story and were claiming that large numbers of tribesmen had been mown down by cannonfire from the ship, while John and the other missionaries sat on board the *Dayspring* watching it all and egging the sailors on. There were even cartoons in which the *Dayspring* was shown hiding behind the man-of-war while cannonballs flew in all directions and heaps of dead bodies were piling up on the shore!

Before John could start holding meetings on behalf of the mission he had to clear his name. He wrote at once to the newspapers, telling his side of the story and threatening legal action for libel if they did not publish an apology as well as a statement withdrawing the charges they had made against the missionaries. Then he appealed to the commodore, who promised his help in stating the true facts of the case.

In time a public enquiry was held into all that had happened and John was called to give evidence at it. The commodore also submitted a report in which he cleared the missionaries of any shadow of blame, or responsibility for the actions he had taken. Reports of all this were published in the newspapers and at last the public interest in the incident began to subside. However, it made John's work of recruiting support for the mission difficult for a long time and he lost some friends as a result of it.

John was convinced that by agreeing to act as interpreter for the commodore he had actually helped to save both lives and property. His conscience was clear before the Lord that he had not done anything of which he need be ashamed, but it took him some time to convince other people of this, even fellow Christians and the leaders of his own mission.

At last, when the outcry over this affair began to die down, John set off once again on a tour of the Australian churches to raise money for the work of the mission, and in particular to encourage the Sunday Schools to accept the responsibility for keeping the *Dayspring* afloat.

Up till this time John had still been supported by, and remained a member of, his home church in Scotland, but during this trip he was officially appointed by the Presbyterian Churches of Australia to represent them as their first missionary to the New Hebrides.

John very much wanted to return to Tanna and take up his work again there, but the other missionaries did not think it was safe for him and his wife and child to go there by themselves. After discussions they decided to send them instead to the smaller island of Aniwa, which was close to Tanna, but where the natives were less hostile. John was very disappointed that he was unable to go back to Tanna, but he knew that the people of Aniwa needed to hear the gospel as well. John accepted it as the Lord's will when he was directed to start work on Aniwa, even though it was not what he personally would have chosen at that time.

To think about

John was forced to leave the island of Tanna, but still longed to see the natives of that island converted. Despite his desire to go back, he took the advice of his brother missionaries and started a new work on the nearby island of Aniwa.

There is a danger that some strong-willed Christians may want their own way in all they do, but John showed his wisdom by listening to the counsel of his colleagues. In Proverbs 11:14 we find the advice: 'Where there is no counsel, the people fall; but in the multitude of counsellors there is safety.'

As Christians we must be ready to listen to the advice of others and at times bow to their wise counsel, even though it might not be what we want. We all need to ask the question: 'I can give advice, but do I listen to the advice of my friends?'

19.
A new beginning

On 8 August 1866 John and Margaret and their baby set sail on the *Dayspring* for Aneityum, on the first stage of their journey to Aniwa and a new beginning in the work of teaching the islanders of the New Hebrides about the Lord Jesus Christ. They were accompanied on the *Dayspring* by three other missionary couples, including John's old friend Joseph Copeland and his wife Elizabeth, all of whom were going out to work on various islands in the group.

When they reached the New Hebrides the *Dayspring* spent a few weeks sailing from one island to another, giving the new missionaries a good look at the whole missionfield as well as collecting those who were already working on the islands, to bring them to Aneityum for a conference at which it was to be finally decided exactly where everyone was to be based.

As the ship sailed around the islands, the natives could scarcely believe their eyes. 'How is this?' they asked one another. 'We killed or drove them all away! We plundered their houses and robbed them. Had we been so treated, nothing would have made us return. But they come back with a beautiful new ship and with more and more missionaries!' What made this all the remarkable was the fact that they knew these men had not come to trade and make money, like the other white men, but to tell them about the Christian God and his Son Jesus. Some of them began to say amongst themselves, 'If their God makes them do all that, we may well worship him too.'

After the mission conference there was a further delay of five weeks before John and Margaret could leave for Aniwa while the *Dayspring* went to the aid of the London Missionary Society's ship the *John Williams*, which had become stuck on a coral reef.

While they were on Aneityum John learned of the death of his faithful old Christian friend Abraham while he had been away on his travels. As he was dying Abraham had asked a friend to look after his watch, which was one of his special treasures, until he could hand it over to John, whom he wanted to have it. 'Give it to Missi, my own Missi Paton,' Abraham said, 'and tell him that I go to Jesus, where time is dead.' John grieved at the loss of a dear friend, but was glad to know that the old man was now with the Lord whom he loved. He knew that the glorious day would come when they would be reunited before the throne of Jesus Christ and, together with all God's people, would praise God for his grace in saving them.

John also shed a tear when he heard that his faithful old guard-dog Clutha had died. He had been forced to leave her behind on the islands, in the care of one of the natives, when he sailed for Australia. After he had gone the dog had fretted for her master and eventually died.

At last John and Margaret boarded the *Dayspring* and sailed for Aniwa. On the way the ship called at Tanna where it sheltered in the harbour for a few days due to bad weather. While they were there old Chief Nowar came out to the ship and tried to persuade them to land and stay on the island, instead of going on to Aniwa.

When the captain of the *Dayspring* told Nowar that he was not allowed to unload John's boxes on Tanna, Nowar said, 'Don't land them. Just throw them over; my men and I will catch everything before it reaches the water, and carry them all safely ashore.'

The captain said he could not do that, so Nowar told him, 'Then just point them out to us. You will have no further trouble; we will manage everything for Missi.'

Nowar did not give up easily. When his ploy to get the couple's boxes taken on shore failed, he persuaded John and his wife to go with him to look over his plantation. There, surrounded by all his growing crops, he turned to Margaret and eagerly told her, 'Plenty of food! While I have a yam or a banana, you shall not want.'

Margaret knew only a few words of Tannese, but with John's help she managed to make him understand that she was not afraid of going short of food.

Nowar evidently thought she was afraid of being attacked by hostile tribesmen, so he pointed next to all his armed warriors standing around them and told her, 'We are many! We are strong! We can always protect you.'

Once again Margaret told him, 'I am not afraid.'

Still Nowar was not going to be beaten. He led the way to the chestnut tree where John had spent the night hiding up in the branches when he was trying to escape from Miaki's men. Pointing up at the tree, Nowar told Margaret, 'The God who protected Missi there will always protect you.'

Margaret, with John acting as interpreter, explained carefully that they must go to Aniwa now, but they hoped one day to return to Tanna if the Lord opened up the way for them to do so. Nowar and his companions seemed really sorry that the missionaries could not stay and this only made the parting even harder for John.

They learnt much later that when Nowar eventually realized that he could not persuade them to stay on Tanna he went to see Pavingin, one of the sacred men from Aniwa who was just then on a visit to Tanna. Nowar took from his own arm the bracelet of white shells which marked him out as a chief and tied it around Pavingin's arm, saying as he did so, 'By these you promise to protect my Missi and his wife and child on Aniwa. Let no evil befall them; or, by this pledge, I and my people will revenge it.'

John and Margaret finally set foot on Aniwa in November 1866. Aniwa was one of the smaller islands in the group, only seven miles long and two miles wide, and completely surrounded by a coral reef. There was no harbour, just a single gap in the coral through which boats could sail. The quayside was simply a collection of large blocks of coral rolled together in one place. In stormy weather these were often blown away and would have to be replaced. There were days of calm, blue sea, but for most of the time the huge waves rolling in from the ocean and breaking on the reef in clouds of white spray set up a continuous loud roar.

There were no really high hills on Aniwa and the highest point was less than 100 metres above sea level. This meant that rain-clouds did not form regularly over the island. Even when it did rain, the water quickly drained away through the light soil and porous coral rock, so drinking water was often in short supply. However, because of the heavy dew and humid atmosphere the island was covered in lush greenery and an abundance of fruit trees.

In a letter to her family Margaret wrote that she thought she was the first white woman ever to land on the island. As she stepped ashore from the boat, watched by all the curious black faces, not one of whom was smiling, she was very relieved when Kanathie, the wife of the Christian teacher from Aneityum who was already working on the island, came to meet her and took her by the hand to help her pick her way across the reef.

Most of the islanders went about naked, but the married women and other older women wore grass aprons or skirts.

The people were very curious about the missionaries, but even more interested in the things they brought with them — the axes, knives, fish-hooks, pieces of calico and blankets.

When Margaret saw some of the natives arriving for worship on the first Sunday, wearing some of the clothes which she and John had handed out as gifts on their arrival, the sight struck her as so funny that she had to hurry out of the building before she burst out laughing. One man arrived, looking very pleased with himself, wearing only a white vest. Another came striding in, with a woman's skirt pinned round his throat and his fingertips just poking out at the bottom! A third was using a native bag as a hat, 'which he took off with quite the air of a gentleman as he entered the door'.

At first John and Margaret made their home in a native hut which had been prepared for them by the local teachers and which also served as the church. This building was one large room, having no doors or windows, but just openings where these would have been. The walls were made of a mixture of sugar-cane leaves and reeds woven together and fixed over a wooden frame. The earth floor was covered with a layer of small pieces of broken white coral which served as a carpet.

A small area was screened off at one end to act as a bedroom for John and Margaret. The other end was piled high with their boxes. The space left in the middle served in the daytime as their living-room and also as the place of worship. At night it was where the group of workers who had come over from Aneityum to help them settle in used to sleep.

Cooking was carried out in the open air, under a tree. The natives all gathered round to watch when John and Margaret sat down to eat their first meal. As there were no chairs, they had to sit on boxes, using the lid of another box as a table.

Remembering what had happened on Tanna and how unhealthy the climate was in the low coastal area, John wanted to find a piece of higher ground to build a house. He saw one spot which he thought would be an ideal site, but the natives refused to let him build there, insisting instead that he use another site about a quarter of a mile inland.

As he began clearing this plot of ground John found a lot of human bones lying about. He learned that the site had been used for cannibal feasts and no one except the sacred men was allowed to touch the mounds of rubbish left behind after these feasts. When John and his companions began work on the site, digging and clearing away the piles of rubbish, the natives watched with great interest to see if the gods would strike them dead.

One day John pointed to two baskets full of bones that he had collected in clearing the land and asked one of the local chiefs, 'How do these bones come to be here?'

The man just shrugged his shoulders and replied, 'Ah, we are not Tanna-men! We don't eat the bones!'

Some years later John was to discover the real reason why the islanders had insisted that he build on that particular site. The old chief Namakei explained: 'When Missi came we saw his boxes. We knew he had blankets and calico, axes and knives, fish-hooks and all such things. We said, "Don't drive him off, else we will lose all these things. We will let him land. But we will force him to live on the sacred plot. Our gods will kill him, and we will divide all that he has amongst the men of Aniwa."'

'But,' the chief went on, 'Missi built his house on our most sacred spot. He and his people lived there, and the gods did not strike. He planted bananas there, and we said, "Now when they eat of these they will all drop down dead, as our fathers assured us, if anyone ate fruit from that ground, except only our sacred men themselves." These bananas ripened. They did eat them. We kept watching for days and days, but no one died! Therefore what we say, and what our fathers have said, is not true. Our gods cannot kill them. Their Jehovah God is stronger than the gods of Aniwa.' So God used even the spot where the mission house was built to convince the islanders that he was the one true God, who ruled in heaven and on earth.

While John was busy building the house, Margaret usually stayed in the hut with the baby and one or two of the native women would keep her company. One day, when she was sitting by herself, she heard a rustling sound coming from behind the curtain where the boxes were stored. She went to lift the curtain and have a look, but at first all she could make out in the gloom was a pair of staring eyes. She dropped the curtain in terror and a moment later it was flung aside by a little man who shouted at her angrily, 'What for you look me?'

'Because I did not know who was there,' Margaret replied.

But the man was not convinced. 'You plenty lie!' he shouted. 'You 'fraid me steal. Me no steal, me come worship. What for you look me steal?'

The man went off to the village and returned soon afterwards with about twenty of his friends. Margaret took little Bobby outside where she sat sewing, trying to look as if nothing was wrong, with the toddler playing at her feet, while the whole crowd of men sat a little distance away watching her. The man she had disturbed among the boxes sat glaring at her the whole time, clutching his club, and every now and again shouting, 'You plenty lie!'

This went on for hours, but when it started to get dark Margaret decided she had had enough. She picked Bobby up and began walking quietly away until she had gone far enough into the bush to be out of sight of the men. Then she ran as fast as she could and never stopped till she reached the spot where John was working. By the time she arrived she was breathless and half-fainting from fright, but little Bobby thought it all great fun and the sound of his laughter echoed through the woods as they ran.

In general, however, they had much less trouble from the natives than in John's early days on Tanna. The Aniwans were not so brazen about stealing things, though they did sometimes swing their tomahawks in a threatening way when they came asking for something they wanted. News of the *Curaçoa*'s visit to Tanna had, of course, reached Aniwa and John heard at least one of the natives warning his friends not to 'murder or to steal, for the man-of-war that punished Tanna would blow up their little island'!

However, there was always a need for care, because the people of Aniwa were cannibals, and violence and revenge were all part and parcel of their lives, as the story of the first Christian workers to come to the island showed only too well.

Many years earlier, before missionaries had come with the gospel to any of the islands, a party of men from Aniwa had made a friendly visit to Aneityum, where all but two[1] of them had been killed and eaten by the natives. The men who escaped hid in the bush, living on coconuts, until they were able to get away one night in a canoe. When they arrived back home in Aniwa and told the dreadful tale of how their companions had all been murdered, the islanders vowed to take revenge.

It was too far — some forty-eight miles — to send a raiding-party to attack the people of Aneityum. So the natives dug a trench in the earth as a visible sign that one day revenge had to be exacted. For almost eighty years the trench was annually cleaned out, as a reminder to the warriors of their duty. Each year a branch from a nearby tree was also placed beside the cut in the earth. As the pile of branches grew taller, so too grew the desire for revenge.

In this way the memory of the murders was kept alive until the time came when two Christian teachers from Aneityum arrived to work in Aniwa. On their arrival the senior island chief, Namakei, promised them protection. However, a problem arose when the islanders realized that these men had come from the island, and even from the very tribe, of their sworn enemies. Namakei did not want to go back on his promise, so the Aniwans hired three men to come over from Tanna to carry out the killing. One of these men had recently seen one of his sons die and he held the missionaries and their God to be responsible.

The three warriors lay in wait for the teachers one Sunday afternoon as they returned from taking the gospel to the surrounding villages. When the teachers approached their hiding-place, the warriors leapt out of the bushes and struck them down with their clubs. In the attack, one teacher was killed and the other, whose name was Navalak, was seriously wounded.

Chief Namakei had the wounded man carried home to his own village and nursed him back to health. The chief managed to persuade his people that honour had been satisfied by the murder of one teacher and the wounding of another in revenge for the killing of the Aniwan warriors eighty years earlier. Navalak was then allowed to return home to his island in peace.

Some time later, when one of the mission ships called at the island, Chief Namakei sent word to Aneityum that the feud was over and that if they sent more teachers these men would be safe and under the chief's protection. The Aniwans were not really interested in hearing the gospel, but they wanted to be on good terms with the people of Aneityum because they knew that trading ships called there, and trading ships meant blankets, mats, baskets and iron tools.

Soon two new Christian teachers and their wives were on their way to Aniwa, where they set up their homes, one at each end of the island. These were the teachers who welcomed John and Margaret on their arrival. However, John soon found that the local people treated them as little better than slaves and they lived in constant fear of their lives.

A number of other helpers had come from Aneityum to help John with the heavy work of clearing the land and building the house. Unfortunately, one day when John was cutting up some wood the axe he was using slipped and he badly cut his ankle. He had to pay the islanders with fish-hooks to carry him back to the hut. Although he carefully dressed the wound it was several weeks before it healed and he was fit enough to do any more work on the house. The workers who had been helping him were all unskilled labourers who had no idea what to do without John there to supervise them. The next time the *Dayspring* called, John had to pay them off and send them back home to Aneityum, with the building work still unfinished, as he and Margaret did not have enough supplies of food to feed them all.

It was hard to find any Aniwans who were willing to help him with the work, even for payment of fish-hooks or lengths of calico, because the men were not used to doing hard work like digging and building. In their culture the men used to stand or sit around and watch while the women did all the work.

Gradually, however, in the months that followed the building work continued and the house rose on its foundations. It was raised up on coral blocks which allowed the cool air to circulate underneath the rooms, while a wide verandah provided plenty of shade. John had a trench dug all round the house which he filled with broken pieces of coral and this served as a drain. To start with there were two main rooms to the house, but others were added over the years. Eventually, when it was finished, it had six rooms opening off a lobby, with a pantry and bath-house under part of the verandah at the back, as well as a storage place for tools. All the main rooms had glass doors, like French windows, which opened onto the verandah. Underneath the house was a cellar which was fitted up with shelves and used for storage. It also served as a shelter whenever hurricanes or cyclones struck the islands. When that

Mission house on Aniwa

happened everyone would squeeze into the cellar, where they would be safe while up above them the wind tore up trees and buildings and tossed them around like feathers or matchsticks.

Over the years a complete little village was to grow up around the mission. Close to the mission house two small homes were built for orphans — one for boys and the other for girls. When John arrived, the hut where he and Margaret lived until their house was ready also served as the church-building and the school, but later a new church and school were built on the higher ground close to the mission house. In time the village even had its own blacksmith's forge and carpenter's workshop, as well as a building for the printing-press, a separate cookhouse and a store for bananas and yams. Roads were laid out, and fences put up and painted. The whole area was surrounded by trees. Along the shoreline there were rows of swaying coconut palms, while spreading chestnuts and fruit trees cast their shade around the house and kept the missionaries and their friends well supplied with breadfruit and bananas — at least until another hurricane came and blew them all down again!

Though the buildings were all very primitive by European standards, the village was a very pleasant place to live, and much healthier than any of the mission stations where John or other missionaries to the islands had lived previously. Over time, the islanders copied what they saw John doing and began building better homes for themselves. As many of them were converted they also developed a new attitude towards work and were glad to offer their time and labour freely for the work of building the church and school.

John had to learn many new skills in order to complete all this work. For example, when lime was needed for plastering the walls of the buildings he had to work out how to make a simple lime kiln. A group of the natives went out to sea in John's boat, dived into the water and, using crowbars and hammers, broke large lumps of coral off the reef and brought the pieces back to land in the boat. Then they dug a large pit and put a pile of dry wood in the bottom. On top of that they spread a layer of fresh, green brushwood that would not easily burn. The coral blocks were laid on top of the brushwood. Then the men set fire to the wood and left the heap to burn slowly for several days until the coral had melted down to lime.

While all this work was going on, John and Margaret were gradually learning the language, using the same method as John had used on Tanna. They asked questions such as 'What is this?' or 'What's your name?' Many of the islanders understood the Tannese language, so John was usually able to make himself understood even in the early days by speaking to them in Tannese. However, he wanted to be able to tell the people about the Lord Jesus, and eventually give them the Scriptures, in their own language.

Every day after lunch they would ring a bell to let the islanders know they were available to give advice and medicine to those who needed it. Those who visited John and Margaret received a very warm welcome, as well as a cup of tea and a piece of bread. As always John took the opportunity to speak about the Lord Jesus Christ to all who came.

1. In the Autobiography John Paton only mentions one survivor, but according to other accounts there were two.

To think about

The natives were amazed that the missionaries who had been so harshly treated should return. This was an act of Christian love which should be seen in the lives of each one who confesses Christ as Lord and Saviour.

The natives were fearful of the power exercised by their wise men. The life of the poor people was governed by superstition and fear of their 'gods'. Today we find the same fears in the hearts of many people as they read their 'stars', consult 'fortune-tellers', refuse to walk under a ladder, suffer nervous stress when a black cat crosses their path or they break a mirror.

John Paton lived with the knowledge that the God of the Bible ruled the universe. We all need to understand the same truth and then we shall not worry about the 'stars' or any of these other things. Our God is working all things for his own glory and the benefit of his people. That truth should be a great encouragement to us all.

20.
Getting to know the people of Aniwa

The language of Aniwa, like that of Tanna, had never been written down before, so every time John learnt a new word, he wrote it down, copying the pronunciation as best he could, and made a note of the way it was used. In this way he soon built up a good vocabulary and was able to make himself understood by the people he met. Of course he also hoped that one day, when he had enough of the language written down, he would be able to translate the Scriptures into the islanders' own language.

One day, when he was building his house, John discovered that he needed more nails and other tools. He picked up a small piece of wood that was smooth enough to write on and wrote a note to Margaret asking her for the things he needed. Then he handed it to the old chief and asked him to take it to Mrs Paton. Namakei stared blankly at John and asked, 'But what do you want?'

'The wood will tell her,' John replied.

The chief must have thought that John was playing a joke on him. He sounded cross as he muttered, 'Whoever heard of wood speaking?'

Eventually John persuaded him to go and, to Namakei's amazement, Margaret looked at the piece of wood and then went to fetch the things that were needed, without his having to say a word. When the chief came back he was very excited and made signs to John asking for an explanation.

John read out to him what he had written on the piece of wood and then explained that God spoke to his people in the same way through a book, the Bible. If the chief learned to read, John told him, he would be able to hear God speaking to him from the page of the book in the same way that Mrs Paton had heard John when she looked at the piece of wood. From that day onward, Namakei was eager to help John learn new words. He could hardly wait for the day when he would be able to hear God speaking to him from the pages of a book.

Another time an old chief from one of the inland villages brought his three sons to watch John at work building the house. They were fascinated by what they saw, but soon afterwards one of the sons fell ill. The father immediately blamed the missionaries and threatened to kill them if the lad died. John treated the young man, giving him medicine, and he recovered. Now the chief could not do too much for John. He began coming to the services and even helped to translate what was said for the local people.

As soon as two of the rooms in the new house were completed John hired two young men to carry boxes up to the house from the native hut where he and Margaret had been living. The men set off carrying a heavy box suspended from a pole which they carried on their shoulders. Soon afterwards both men became ill and one of them died. Again the missionaries were blamed and the father of the second man warned that if his son died too he would kill everyone at the mission in revenge. Once again God intervened and the man recovered.

John decided after this that he needed an easier and safer way of transporting goods the three-quarters of a mile up to the house from the boat-landing. He could not risk any more men falling ill after carrying loads for him! So John racked his brains and designed a simple home-made wheelbarrow which they used until he was able to get a proper hand-cart from Australia. He also set about persuading the natives to help him construct a road, which they surfaced with small broken pieces of white coral.

However, not everyone welcomed the missionaries. There were threats to set fire to the new mission house before it was even completed, but when Chief Namakei heard of these threats he ordered some of his people to keep watch day and night and to protect John and Margaret and their helpers.

For about ten days a warrior who was on a visit from the island of Erromanga, armed with a musket and a tomahawk, followed John around wherever he went. At first John quietly went on with his work as if nothing was wrong, but when the man did not go away he sent for the chief with whom the warrior was staying and warned him that if any of the missionaries were killed God would hold the chief responsible.

The chief was quick to reassure John that he knew nothing about the man's evil intentions. 'Missi,' he said, 'I did not know. I did not know. But by the first favourable wind he shall go, and you will see him no more.' The chief was as good as his word and the man was sent away. Once again God had protected his servants.

The tribesmen would not usually dare to attack anyone openly while the person was watching. Often John was able to avert an attack at the last moment by rushing straight into the arms of a warrior who was in the very act of swinging his club in the air or pointing his gun. He would seize the man's arms and hold them tightly so that he could not move until his temper cooled down enough to allow John to release his grip and slip away unharmed.

When John and Margaret first arrived on the island they found that the Christian teachers from Aneityum who were already there held a worship service each Lord's Day in their

John several times had to seize a warrior by the arms and restrain him
until his temper cooled

own language. A number of the islanders would come along, but they did not pay attention to the service, most of which they probably could not understand since it was in the Aneityumese language. Instead they would lie around in groups smoking or talking among themselves until the service was over. Then they would all join in the feast which the teachers had been hard at work preparing for the last two days.

It was obvious that most of the natives only came for the food. When John arrived on Aniwa he quickly put an end to these weekly feasts and many of them stopped coming to the services. Some of them even demanded food or other things as payment for coming to worship. John would have none of that. He was not going to bribe people to come to the services!

As soon as they had mastered enough of the language John began visiting the villages, usually accompanied by one of the teachers and one or two of the local people who were friendly. They spoke to the villagers about the Lord Jesus and invited them to come to the services. In fine weather these were held in the open under a banyan tree, but if it was raining they used a hut built by the natives. The missionaries also gradually gained the confidence of the local people by showing them kindness.

One of the first people they got to know was Chief Namakei, who owned the land surrounding the spot where they were living. He often came to visit them at the mission house, especially when they were having a meal. He would come regularly, morning and evening, for a cup of tea and a piece of bread. When they first offered him a cup of tea he tasted it and then passed the cup around among the people who had come with him so they could all have a taste of the white people's drink. At first John thought he came mainly for the tea, but after a while Namakei became really interested in what the missionaries told him about the Lord Jesus. Soon he was bringing along his friend Chief Naswai and Naswai's wife

Katua. All three of them came to know and love the Lord Jesus as their Saviour. John and Margaret had the joy of seeing the great change in their lives as they learned more about the Bible and the way Christians should live.

Namakei did not have a son of his own, only a daughter, Litsi. When another son was born to John and Margaret, soon after they moved into their new home, Namakei wanted to name the baby after himself and to make him his heir. He kept bringing people to the house to have a look at 'the white chief of Aniwa', as he called the baby (even though John and Margaret decided to call him Fred and not Namakei!). When Fred learned to walk, Namakei would take him by the hand and walk about with him to meet all the people, talking to him all the while in his own native language. Soon the little boy could speak the chief's language. This really helped to break down any remaining barriers between the islanders and the family at the mission house, paving the way for the people to come to the mission to be taught about the Lord Jesus.

In fact John and Margaret were to find that their family life was to play an important part in their Christian witness on the island. When, a couple of years later, they had a little girl (whom they always called Minn), the native women who came to see the new baby at first thought that Margaret would be very upset over the birth of a baby girl, because their culture only valued sons. But after Margaret had showed them the baby and told them how pleased she was to have a daughter, they went away very excited because they had seen 'a real little white woman of Aniwa'. Margaret later wrote to her family that the attitude of many natives changed towards baby girls as a result of seeing how much she and John loved their little girl, and valued her as a precious gift from God. 'All little girls of Aniwa will be more lovingly treated in the days to come, for the love we showed to this Little Woman of Aniwa,' she told them.

Namakei also brought his daughter Litsi to the missionaries and said he wanted her to live with them: 'I want to leave my Litsi with you. I want to train her for Jesus.' She was an intelligent child and soon became a real help to Margaret. Then her uncle Kalangi also brought his little girl along to be trained like her cousin. The girls told their fathers about what they saw at the mission house and this soon led to the adults taking an interest in the gospel. These two girls were only the first of many children who were to be brought to John and Margaret for training and for whom they were to act as foster-parents in the years ahead. Margaret took particular responsibility for the girls and they learned to help her about the house and with the children. John trained the boys to help him in his work. As well as learning practical tasks such as building, a number of them went on to become native teachers for the mission.

Often it was these children who warned John and Margaret when there were plans afoot to kill or harm them. When some of the villagers gave up worshipping their idols, the other natives, who resented the 'new religion', decided to set fire to the mission house. John noticed piles of large coconut leaves around the house each morning but did not know why they were there. Then one night Namakei woke John, calling out, 'Rise, Missi, and help! The heathen are trying to burn your house. All night we have kept them off, but they are many and we are few. Rise quickly, and light a lamp at every window. Let us pray to Jehovah, and talk loud as if we were many. God will make us strong.'

John went outside to find the chief and his people, together with the teachers, standing ready with pails of water while all around in the bush figures could be soon moving carrying lighted torches. He then found out that the natives had been guarding the house every night while the family slept and they had been using the coconut leaves as umbrellas to protect them from the heavy overnight dew while they stood outside keeping guard. John wanted to take his turn with them in keeping watch, but after they had talked it over among themselves they would not let him because of the risk that he might be hurt. 'If our Missi is shot or killed in the dark, what will we have to watch for then?' they asked. So John was told to stay indoors after dark!

One morning a man named Tupa came running up to the house. He was very excited and as soon as he came near enough shouted out, 'Missi, I have killed the Tebil! I have killed Teapolo. He came to catch me last night. I raised all the people, and we fought him round the house with our clubs. At daybreak he came out and I killed him dead. We will have no more bad conduct or trouble now. Teapolo is dead!'

John knew that 'Teapolo' was their word for 'devil', so he answered, 'What nonsense! Teapolo is a spirit, and cannot be seen.'

When the man insisted that he really had killed the Teapolo Margaret suggested that John should go with him to see what he was talking about. The man led John to a lump of coral regarded by the islanders as a sacred rock, and showed him the body of a huge sea-serpent. 'There he lies!' said Tupa. 'Truly I killed him.'

'That is not the devil,' John told him. 'It is only the body of a serpent.'

'Well, but it is all the same!' Tupa answered at once. 'He is Teapolo. He makes us bad, and causes all our troubles.'

John found out that the superstitious natives worshipped the serpent as a spirit of evil, whom they called Matshiktshiki. They lived in terror of this spirit and believed that somehow it was responsible for all their troubles and sufferings. Their religious sacrifices and rituals were meant to pacify the spirit and turn away his anger. John was reminded of the account in the Bible of the Fall, when Satan appeared to Adam and Eve in the form of a snake, and thought that the traditions handed down to the islanders from their ancestors were based on a distorted version of this true story.

As God worked in the hearts of men and women, turning them away from their heathen ways to a life of love for, and trust in, the Lord Jesus, they began to give up their superstitious and cruel pagan customs, which included killing young children, or wives who dared to oppose their husbands' wishes. John and the other missionaries spoke out very strongly against these cruel practices. In time they had the joy of seeing several of those who had once committed murders or other terrible crimes truly repenting of their sins and coming regularly to join in the worship around the Lord's Table.

War and killing for revenge had been so much part of the way of life for these people that this was the area of their lives where the changes were most noticeable when they were brought to believe in Christ and sought to follow him. After they became Christians the two chiefs Namakei and Naswai would often tell their people, 'We are the men of Christ now. We must not fight. We must put down murders and crimes among our people.'

There were still a number who were strongly opposed to the missionaries and the worship of God. Some of them tried to provoke the new Christians to fight. One old chief made a point of openly working on building his canoe on the Lord's Day as a deliberate gesture of defiance against the Christians. After a time the man became ill and his brother arrived one Sunday during the service, accompanied by a crowd of armed men, trying to start a fight. However, the converted natives refused to be drawn into taking up arms. Even when one of them was struck with a club he did not retaliate, but said he would leave his revenge to the Lord.

Another time the chiefs held a meeting at which a few men tried to persuade the rest to burn down the mission house and drive out the missionaries or kill them. After some discussion Pavingin, the sacred man who had been on Tanna when the *Dayspring* called there with John and Margaret on their way to Aniwa, stood up and told the story of how Nowar had pressed his chief's bracelet on him and made him promise to protect 'the Missi' from harm, or else the men from Tanna would come and punish them! That settled it: the meeting decided to leave 'the Missi' alone!

When John noticed one of the warriors hanging around day after day watching him as he worked on the house, he began to feel uneasy, especially since this was the man who had once given Margaret such a fright after she found him among the boxes in their old hut. Seeing the man standing so close, with his tomahawk in his hand, John asked him, 'Nelwang, do you want to speak to me?'

'Yes, Missi,' the warrior replied. 'If you will help me now, I will be your friend for ever.'

When John asked, 'Well, how can I help you?' Nelwang replied, 'I want to get married, and I need your help.'

At first John could not see how he could help, since marriages were all arranged when the children were still very young, and to try to interfere would be asking for trouble. However, Nelwang explained that he wanted to marry Yakin, who was the widow of a chief who had died, and who was therefore free to marry again.

John then asked, 'Do you know if she loves you or would take you?'

'Yes,' replied Nelwang. 'One day I met her on the path and told her I would like to have her for my wife. She took out her ear-rings and gave them to me... I was one of her late husband's men, and if she had loved any of them more than she loved me, she would have given them to another. With the ear-rings she gave me her heart.'

'Then why,' asked John, 'don't you go and marry her?'

Nelwang explained the problem: 'In her village there are thirty young men for whom there are no wives. Each of them wants her, but no one has the courage to take her, for the other twenty-nine will shoot him!' He was sure that if he tried to marry her, all thirty of the warriors would turn on him and kill him. He asked John what he would do, if he were in Nelwang's place.

After they had discussed it for a while, John advised that the best plan would be for the couple to elope! With the help of a couple of his friends who were sworn to secrecy, Nelwang, in the dead of night, broke through the fence surrounding Yakin's house and carried her off into the bush to marry her.

When the other warriors discovered both Nelwang and Yakin had disappeared they were very angry. They broke down the fences round both their houses and began destroying their property. After this had gone on for a couple of days John appeared on the scene, while the men were feasting on Nelwang's crops. He asked Chief Naswai, 'What's this your men are about?... I can get no peace to study, or carry on my work.'

The chief duly explained: 'Nelwang has eloped with Yakin.'

'Oh,' said John, 'is that all? Call your men and let me speak to them.'

John then turned to the young men and asked, 'After all your kindness to Yakin ... has she really run away and left you all? Don't you feel thankful that you are free from such an ungrateful woman?... Are you really making all this noise over such a person, and destroying so much useful food?' Soon the warriors were agreeing that Yakin was not worth so much trouble, and that Nelwang would be sufficiently punished by having such a woman as his wife!

Some weeks later, during which time nothing had been heard from the runaways, Nelwang found John when he was working by himself and told him, 'I come now to fulfil my promise: I will help you, and Yakin will help Missi Paton the woman, and we shall be your friends.'

He asked if they could come and live with John and his family until the fuss had all died down and it was safe for them to set up home on their own. John agreed and they arrived the next day. Yakin was a great help to Margaret around the house and Nelwang followed John around like his shadow! They also began to show a real interest in the gospel and in time both became true Christians and valued members of the church. Yakin went on to become a Sunday School teacher and used to lead the singing in church when Margaret was unable to attend.

After they had been at the mission-house a few weeks John encouraged them both to appear publicly at the worship service. Other people would have to learn to accept them as man and wife and the sooner they were seen together in public the better. It was an occasion he was never to forget.

Nelwang waited till the very last minute, when the bell announcing the service had stopped ringing and everyone else was already in their seats. Then he walked in, smartly dressed in shirt and kilt, and, still clutching his tomahawk, sat down as close to John as he could.

A few moments later Yakin entered. She had evidently decided to dress in style for the occasion, since pagans wore no clothes and adopting Western dress was recognized among the natives as a sign of becoming a Christian. So she put on every article of clothing she could lay her hands on! Over her grass skirt she wore a man's overcoat which reached down to her ankles. On top of that she wore a vest, and her head and shoulders protruded from the seat of a pair of man's trousers, with the two empty trouser-legs dangling down either side in front of her. She had also fastened a red shirt to one shoulder and a striped one to the other, and these flapped like wings as she walked along. Another red shirt was wound round her head like a turban, with a sleeve hanging down over each ear. John said afterwards she looked like 'a moving monster loaded with a mass of rags'. The sight of her sitting sweltering in the heat under the weight of all those clothes made him keep the service as short as he could. He said it was probably the shortest service he had ever conducted in his life!

Nelwang, however, smiled lovingly at the vision of beauty before his eyes and then looked at John with an expression of pride, as if to say, 'You never saw ... a bride so grandly dressed!'

To think about

Holiness is the way of life expected of God's people. That means obedience to the laws of God. Christ said, 'You are my friends if you do whatever I command you' (John 15:14).

John found that the islanders had picked up bad habits from their contact with traders. There is a warning here for all Christians: beware of the influence of the godless people of the world. Just have a look around you and you will see the influence of the world upon you. Have a look at the multitude of material possessions that have a place in your life. In the West, pleasure and sport are the gods of this age.

Satan is waiting to use anything he can to cause Christians to fall into sin. This means we need to be on guard at all times. It also means we need to know what the Bible teaches so we can obey the commands of Christ.

What aspects of your life are dragging you down spiritually and what are you going to do to overcome the difficulty?

21.
God's 'rain' comes up from the ground!

John and Margaret found the shortage of fresh water a real problem. As we saw earlier, the island had very little rain and most of what did fall was quickly lost. The rainy season was from December to April and for the rest of the year water was in very short supply. This did not worry the islanders too much as they mainly drank the juice from coconuts (which looked and tasted something like lemonade), or chewed pieces of sugar-cane when they were thirsty. They only needed very little water for their cooking. When it came to washing, they bathed in the sea and never troubled about washing clothes at all!

John prepared two large casks to store water in, but when they tried to fill these at the local water-hole during the rainy season the villagers would not let them, saying their casks would take all the water and there would be none left for anyone else.

Besides, the water-hole was under the control of the local sacred men, who claimed that they had the power to bring rain to fill the hole, or to stop it from raining. The islanders brought them presents to make it rain, and if no rain came the sacred men would simply demand larger gifts in order to satisfy their gods! In this way they had a very real power over the lives of the villagers. John saw that if there was another source of water

over which they clearly had no control this would help to break
the hold they had on the islanders. He wanted to show the
natives that it was the Christian God who was in control of
everything and supplied food, water and other good things —
not the false gods of the sacred men.

So John decided to try to sink a well near the mission
buildings. He asked God to guide him to the right spot, where
there was an underground spring, and made calculations based
on his observation of the rocks and soil. He had, of course,
some idea as to how to proceed from his earlier experience of
digging a well on Tanna.

One day he told the two chiefs, Namakei and Naswai, 'I am
going to sink a deep well down into the earth, to see if our God
will send us fresh water up from below.'

The men looked at him as if he was mad. 'O Missi!' one of
them told him, 'Rain comes only from above. How could you
expect our island to send up showers of rain from below?'

When John tried to explain that fresh water did indeed
spring up out of the ground in his own country, they told him,
'O Missi, your head is going wrong ... or you would not talk
like that! Don't let our people hear you talking about going
down into the earth for rain, or they will never listen to your
word or believe you again!'

However, John was not to be put off! He carefully chose a
spot near a public path, where the well could be used by all the
villagers, and set to work with pick-axe, spade and bucket,
leaving a ladder and other tools nearby, ready for when he
would need them. The natives came to watch him, thinking he
would soon get tired and give up!

The work really was tiring, especially in the hot sun, so after
a little while John went back into the house and came out with
a pocketful of large fish-hooks. Holding one of them up for the
young men to see, he called out, 'One of these to every man
who fills and turns over three buckets out of this hole!' Now

there was a rush to take a turn at handling the bucket, and the hole in the ground began to grow deeper, until one evening when they stopped for the night John was pleased to see that they had gone down nearly four metres. However, the next morning they found that the wall of the pit had collapsed, filling the hole with earth.

After that the natives were convinced that John was mad, and none of them would go down into the hole to help him, not even for the sake of fish-hooks! The old chief came to John and told him, 'Now, had you been in that hole last night, you would have been buried, and a man-of-war would have come from Queen 'Toria to ask for the Missi who lived here. We would have to say, "He is down in that hole." The captain would have asked, "Who killed him and put him down there? ... Who ever heard of a white man going down into the earth to bury himself? You killed him, you put him down there..." Then he would bring out his big guns and shoot us, and destroy our island in revenge. You are making your own grave, Missi, and you will make ours too... Will you not give it up now?'

However, John told them that he believed his God would supply water and he meant to persevere, with God's help, whether they helped him or not. He then rigged up a home-made pulley, using tree-trunks and wooden beams to take the weight. One of the native teachers stood at the top of the pit to empty the bucket when it came up full of earth and to lower it down again. John took a little bell down with him as he worked. When the bucket was full he would ring the bell as the signal to pull it up. The teacher paid some of the young men with axes and knives to take a turn at hauling on the end of the rope till the bucket rose to the surface.

In this way John finally reached a depth of about ten metres below the earth — approximately the depth that he had originally calculated. He noticed that the soil and rocks at this level were damp and, believing that God had indeed guided him to a source of water in answer to his prayers, he told the chief that night, 'I think that Jehovah God will give us water tomorrow from that hole.'

Still the chief was sure it would not work. 'No, Missi,' he said, 'you will never see rain coming up from the earth on this island… We expect daily, if you reach water, to see you drop through into the sea, and the sharks will eat you! That will be the end of it — death to you and danger to us all.'

But John told him, 'Come tomorrow. I hope and believe that Jehovah God will send you the rainwater up through the earth.'

John knew he was taking a risk in saying this, but he believed God was leading him in the search for water and was confident that God would answer his prayers because his own honour was at stake. He also thought of the water as a symbol of the 'living water' that the Lord Jesus had spoken about to the woman at the well in John's Gospel. He prayed that God would not only give the islanders water to drink, but that he would pour out his Spirit on them and give them the even more precious gift of eternal life.

Early the next morning, just as the sun was rising, John went back to the well and made a small hole in the centre of the shaft. He was trembling with excitement as water started to bubble up from the hole. He tasted it and, yes, it was fresh water! John almost went down on his knees right there in the hole; he was so full of praise and thanks to God who had sent him water.

Meanwhile the chiefs and their men had gathered round to watch. When John had calmed down a little and the mud had had time to settle, he filled a jug with the water and, climbing up the ladder to the top, held it out to them, telling them to come and see the rain that God had given them by means of the well.

The old chief took the jug from John's hand, shook it to see if it would spill, touched the water with his finger to see if it felt wet and finally tasted a sip. After rolling it around in his mouth to get the full flavour of the water, he swallowed it and exclaimed, 'Rain! Rain! Yes, it's rain! But how did you get it?'

'Jehovah my God gave it out of his own earth in answer to our labours and prayers,' John told him. 'Go and see it springing up for yourselves.'

That was easier said than done! Even though all the men watching were fearless warriors who thought nothing of climbing up into a tree like a monkey, none of them had the courage to come to the edge of the well and lean over to look down! But then they thought of a solution. They all stood in a line, one behind the other, and linked hands. The man at the front carefully bent over to have a look, while all the others held on to him from behind. Then he ran to the back of the queue, to let the next man take a look, and so on until they had all had a turn to gaze down at the precious, life-giving water bubbling up through the earth.

The chief then turned to John and exclaimed, 'Missi, wonderful, wonderful is the work of your Jehovah God! No god of Aniwa ever helped us in this way.'

Now the men were full of questions: 'Will it always rain up through the earth, or will it come and go like the rain from the clouds? ... Will you or your family drink it all, or shall we also have some?' When John told them he was sure there would always be plenty for all of them, they could hardly believe it: 'Then ... it will be our water, and we may all use it as our very own?'

John told them that the water would always continue there for their use, as a good gift from God. 'You and all your people,' he assured the chief, 'may come and drink and carry away as much of it as you wish. I believe there will always be plenty for us all, and the more of it we can use the fresher it will be. That is the way with many of our Jehovah's best gifts to men, and for it and for all we praise his name!'

Each in turn had a look down the well while the others held on to him
from behind

All the time John had been digging the well no one could be found to help him, but now the cry went up: 'Missi, what can we do to help you now?'

John suggested they all went to the shore and brought back the largest coral blocks they could lay their hands on. They all went rushing off, shouting and singing in their excitement, and soon came struggling back under the weight of enormous blocks of coral which had been washed ashore after the hurricanes. John used these to build a solid wall, nearly a metre thick, lining the sides of the well-shaft so that there would be no more danger of the sides giving way and earth falling into the well and blocking it.

After he had built it up a little over halfway, John was growing very weary and his hands were so sore from handling the rocks that he decided to take a rest for a few days. However, the chief had a better idea: 'Missi ... just point out where each block is to be laid. We will lay them there; we will build them solidly behind like you. And no man will sleep till it is done.' Men, women and children all set to work, carrying and cutting the blocks and fitting them into place until the wall was completed. Finally, when John had covered the opening with wooden boards and set up the bucket and winding-gear, the well was ready to use.

John was glad that all the villagers wanted to use the well because if they were going to drink from it themselves there would be no danger of anyone poisoning it! That well served the island for many years. The level of the water rose and fell with the tides, but it never ran dry and the water was always good to drink. Many years later one of the elders of the church was to tell John, 'But for that water, during the last two years of drought, we would all have been dead!'

Later on, several attempts were made to sink other wells in different parts of the island, but none of them was successful. The islanders used to say to each other, 'Missi not only used pick and spade, but he prayed and cried to his God. We have learned to dig, but not how to pray, and therefore Jehovah will not give us the rain from below!'

When the work on the well was finished, Chief Namakei said to John, 'Missi, I think I could help you next Sabbath. Will you let me preach a sermon on the well?'

John agreed and the next Lord's Day a large crowd came along to the service, eager to hear what their chief had to say. Namakei arrived, smartly dressed in shirt and kilt and, after John had opened the service with prayer, he rose to his feet, swinging his tomahawk in the air every time he made a point.

'Friends of Namakei,' he began, 'men and women and children of Aniwa, listen to my words! Since Missi came here he has talked many strange things we could not understand — things all too wonderful; and we said regarding many of them that they must be lies… But of all his wonderful stories, we thought the strangest was about sinking down through the earth to get rain!' He reminded them how they had thought John was mad when he told them his God would give him rain from the earth. 'We mocked at him,' Namakei went on, 'but the water was there all the same. We have laughed at other things which the Missi told us, because we could not see them. But from this day I believe that all he tells us about his Jehovah God is true. Some day our eyes will see it. For today we have seen the rain from the earth.'

If they had not seen it with their own eyes, nothing in the world, Namakei continued, would have made them believe that rain could come from the depths of the earth. Then, thumping his chest as he spoke, he went on to tell his hearers: 'Something here in my heart tells me that Jehovah God does exist, the Invisible One, whom we never heard of nor saw till the Missi brought him to our knowledge.' Just as the water had been there all the time, though their eyes could not see it, he declared, 'so I, your chief, do now firmly believe that when I die ... I shall ... see the invisible Jehovah God with my soul, as Missi tells me, not less surely than I have seen the rain from the earth below. From this day, my people, I must worship the God who has opened for us the well, and who fills us with rain from below. The gods of Aniwa cannot hear, cannot help us, like the God of Missi. Henceforth I am a follower of Jehovah God.'

He then urged his hearers to go and fetch their idols, the pagan gods their fathers had worshipped, and bring them to John to be burnt and destroyed, once and for all. Then, he said, 'Let us be taught by the Missi how to serve the God who can hear, the Jehovah who gave us the well, and who will give us every other blessing, for he sent his Son Jesus to die for us and bring us to heaven...' He concluded by saying, 'The Jehovah God has sent us rain from the earth. Why should he not also send us his Son from heaven? Namakei stands up for Jehovah!'

That very afternoon the chief himself and several of his men arrived at the mission house bringing the idols from their homes to be destroyed. In the weeks that followed one group after another appeared, carrying the idols of wood and stone which they and their fathers had worshipped, and threw them down in piles by the door of the mission house. They made a huge bonfire of everything that could be burnt and those that would not burn were buried in pits deep underground, or even dumped out at sea, where no one would ever find them again.

Of course, not all who brought their idols were truly converted and some even tried to sell the gods to the missionaries and went off in a huff when they refused. But there was a real and growing interest in the Christian worship and people wanted to come and hear about the life and death of the Lord Jesus. Before long any family where they did not make a practice of thanking God for their food and asking his blessing on every meal, or where they did not hold family worship each morning and evening, was branded by the others as 'heathen'!

Wearing clothes had always been recognized as an outward sign of becoming a Christian and now everyone began to wear them. They also began to observe Sunday as the Lord's Day and no ordinary work would be done on that day. In fact Saturday came to be known as 'Cooking Day', because of the extra cooking and other work done on that day in order to leave Sunday free of such tasks.

The influence of the gospel and the teaching of the Bible could be seen in every aspect of life on the island. As they became Christians people also began to work harder and were eager to learn to read. Grandparents and parents, as well as children, would all go to the mission school together, and all learn their alphabet at the same time!

People were no longer afraid of leaving their property behind at home in case it should be stolen. Up till now church services had often been disrupted by the barking of dogs, the squeals of piglets or the clucking of fowls, which their owners had brought along with them, because they dared not leave them behind. Now, as God worked in their hearts, the islanders themselves decided this had to stop. They called a meeting at which they condemned all stealing and worked out a simple system of fines and other punishments, to be administered by their own chiefs, who were to ensure that law and order were maintained.

Two of the former sacred men, together with some other men who were generally respected by the islanders, also formed a kind of committee to make sure that people really had given up the worship of idols and were not still hiding any of them.

Of course, all these things took time and no doubt there were some who, for a while at least, continued to mix some of their old superstitions with their new-found faith. Yet, although no one was compelled to attend church, the time came when everyone on the island, without exception, claimed to worship and serve the true God.

John, Margaret and the other Christians were full of praise and thanks to God, who had been pleased to reveal his truth to these pagan islanders and had sent his Holy Spirit to work in their hearts, bringing about such a wonderful change in their lives. All the praise was due to God alone!

To think about

John was a man of faith. He did not just dig a well, but prayed and dug a well, and God answered his prayer. What do we learn from this incident?

In our culture we are used to the idea of people digging wells and drawing water from them, so we do not see anything very remarkable about it, but to the natives it appeared to be a miracle from the hand of the Lord. God uses simple things to achieve great ends and this is one such instance.

I feel sure that there are not too many people today who would put God to such a test? Why not?

Think about your prayer life and consider the times God has answered your prayers. What do you do if you pray for many years for a particular thing to happen, but nothing happens?

22.
Day-to-day life on Aniwa

The sinking of the well and Namakei's sermon marked a real turning-point in John and Margaret's work on Aniwa, but there was still much work to be done. One of the most pressing tasks was to produce portions of God's Word and hymns in the Aniwan language.

John's own printing-press had been destroyed when he was forced to escape from Tanna, but he had been able to lay his hands on what was left of the one that had belonged to the Gordons, the couple who were murdered on Erromanga. Parts of the press were missing and he had to make replacements out of scraps of iron and wood. Even then he had so few copies of each letter of the alphabet that he could only print four pages at a time. However, John persevered and eventually he was able to print a small hymn-book and part of the book of Genesis in the Aniwan language, as well as a number of booklets.

The first booklet to be printed was a selection of short passages of Scripture, intended as an introduction to the Bible for the islanders. Chief Namakei was a great help to John in translating the text and day after day he would come to John and ask, 'Missi, is it done? Can it speak?'

At last one day John was able to answer, 'Yes!'

'Does it speak my words?' Namakei wanted to know.

When John replied that it did, the old man begged him, 'Make it speak to me, Missi! Let me hear it speak!'

As John started to read aloud from the book, Namakei was so excited that he shouted, 'It does speak! It speaks my own language, too! Oh, give it to me!'

John handed the book to him. The old man turned it over and looked at it from all sides, inside and out. He was puzzled. At last, he handed it back to John saying, very sadly, 'Missi, I cannot make it speak! It will never speak to me!'

'No,' John explained. 'You don't know how to read it yet, how to make it speak to you; but I will teach you to read, and then it will speak to you as it does to me.'

Namakei could not wait to learn. 'O Missi, dear Missi, show me how to make it speak!' he begged.

John soon guessed there was another problem too. He noticed the way Namakei was peering at the book and suspected that he could not make out the letters properly because his eyesight was poor. Fortunately, John was able to help. He had a collection of simple reading glasses which had been sent out for use among the natives. Sorting through the box, he eventually found just the pair for Chief Namakei. At first the old man hesitated about putting them on, in case there were some kind of sorcery involved, but when at last the glasses were firmly in place on his nose, he exclaimed, 'I see it all now! This is what you told us about Jesus. He opened the eyes of a blind man. The word of Jesus has just come to Aniwa. He has sent me these glass eyes! I have got back again the sight that I had when a boy. O Missi, make the book speak to me now!'

John then led him outside, drew the letters A, B and C in the dust and then showed him the same letters in the book. After a little while, Namakei came running in to John saying he had those three letters in his head now, and asking for three more. So it went on until he had learned the whole alphabet and could begin to pick out whole words. He kept asking John to read parts of the book to him and before long he had learnt it all by heart. He used to encourage all the young people to learn to read by telling them, 'If an old man like me has done it, it ought to be much easier for you.'

Namakei's wife Yauwaki was very nervous about going anywhere near the mission house or being expected to learn anything. However, one day she ventured as far as the doorway while Margaret was playing on her little portable organ, or harmonium, and singing a hymn in the Aniwan language. As she sang, Yauwaki gradually crept closer, listening intently. Suddenly she ran off, but it was only to call the other women and girls to come and 'hear the box sing'! From then onwards, the women flocked to the mission house whenever they heard the sound of Margaret singing and playing.

John himself was not at all musical, so he was really thankful that Margaret was talented in that way and able to lead the singing, both in family worship and in the services. Without her musical gifts there would have been no music in the services and he believed the singing of praise to God was an important part of the worship.

One day Namakei and Yauwaki came together to the mission and the chief asked John, 'Missi, can you give my wife also a pair of new glass eyes like mine? She tries to learn, but she cannot see the letters. She tries to sew, but she pricks her finger, and throws away the needle, saying, "The ways of the white people are not good!" If she could get a pair of glass eyes, she would be in a new world like Namakei.'

John looked in his box and found a pair of glasses for Yauwaki. She was scared of putting them on, but when at last she did, she was thrilled: 'Oh, my new eyes! my new eyes!' she exclaimed. 'I have the sight of a little girl. I will learn hard now. I will make up for lost time.' Though she was never very good at reading or sewing, Yauwaki came to be a real help to John and Margaret as she taught the younger women and girls about the Lord Jesus and encouraged all of them to come along to the mission.

When John decided it was time to think about a proper church building, rather than just the native hut they had used for the services at first, he called the islanders together and encouraged them to build it themselves, out of love for the Lord. He would help and advise them, of course, but he did not want them just to expect the missionaries to always go on doing everything for them. They held meetings at which the men made long speeches and waved their clubs and tomahawks about a great deal. Then they all went off to cut down trees, while the women and children began collecting sugarcane for the thatched roof. Tree-trunks were used for the frame of the building, and to support the roof, and the floor was covered with pieces of white coral. The congregation sat on the floor, on mats made from coconut palm leaves, and John's pulpit was a wooden desk on a small platform surrounded by reeds. On the opposite side there was a seat also made from reeds for Margaret to sit on while she played her harmonium.

They were all delighted with the new building. However, when a hurricane struck the island it was completely destroyed. Everyone was very upset, but after a little while the chief stood up and told the people, 'Let us not weep, like boys over their broken bows and arrows! Let us be strong, and build a yet stronger church for Jehovah.'

So they set to work once more. They rescued everything they could from the wreck of the old building and the work was shared out equally among the different villages. One chief at first did not want to take part until John went to see him and told him that the others would hold it against him afterwards if he and his people did not do their share of the work.

After some time, they ran out of large pieces of timber for the roof-beams and work came to a stop until they could find another tree-trunk. One morning John and the family woke up

The church on Aniwa

to the sound of singing and shouting. They looked out and saw a party of men approaching, led by the chief who at first had not wanted to join in the work. The chief was dancing, singing and beating time with his tomahawk, as he walked in front of his men, who were carrying on their shoulders a huge tree-trunk, all blackened by soot. Since no other wood was to be found, the chief had lifted the roof-beam out of his own house, where it had been blackened from the smoke of the fire, and was bringing it to finish the church!

Once more coral was burnt to make lime for plastering the walls and soon the building was complete and ready for worship. A friend from England had sent out a large church bell as a gift and the islanders were very keen to have this put up. Another tree-trunk was cut down and carried, in relays, the half-mile from the shore. The triumphal procession was led by two chiefs waving their tomahawks and leading the rest in a song as they walked. The bell was fixed to the top of the tree-trunk, which was then lowered into a hole in the ground. Finally, they put coral blocks all round the base and cemented them together with lime so that the post was secured firmly.

The first Lord's Supper was held on Aniwa on 24 October 1869. About 180 people attended the service in all, but John had to be sure that those who were admitted to the membership of the church and allowed to sit down at the Lord's Table were really true followers of the Lord Jesus Christ and understood what they were doing. It was, therefore, only those who had first regularly attended special classes and had given John good reason to believe that they were now true Christians who were allowed to take part in the communion.

At that first service twelve of the islanders, including Chief Namakei and his daughter Litsi, were baptized after they had each publicly declared in front of all the congregation their faith in the Lord Jesus as their Saviour, and their desire to live for him and serve him. Then they sat down with John,

Margaret and the other Christian workers to take the bread and wine and remember the death of the Lord Jesus in the way that he had himself commanded. John said afterwards that the moment when he put the bread and the cup which symbolized the love of Christ into the hands of men who had once been cannibals was one of the happiest of his life and a real foretaste of the joy of heaven. It made all the hardships and difficulties of the last few years worthwhile!

That afternoon a prayer meeting was held in the open air under the shade of a large banyan tree and seven of the new church members took part in leading the others in prayer. After each prayer they joined together in singing hymns of praise.

John described a typical Lord's Day on the island. The family would get up at daybreak and have breakfast. Then it was time to ring the church bell for the first service of the day. While the bell was ringing everyone would take their places in church and by the time it stopped all the members of the congregation were in their seats. There were no late-comers to the services on Aniwa! The service lasted about an hour, then, after a break of about twenty minutes, the bell would be rung again and a second service would be held. John usually asked one of the native Christians to lead in prayer during each of these services and it was a real encouragement to everyone to hear these men who had once been idol-worshippers praying and praising the Lord in their own language.

After the second service there would be two strokes on the bell. This was the signal for the class to begin for those who were seeking to join the church as new members. They would normally stay in this class for anything up to two years, during which time John instructed them carefully from the church catechism in all the central teachings of the Christian faith. Only after that were they allowed to join the membership of the church and take part in the Lord's Supper.

While this class was going on, those who were already church members met for a time of prayer in the nearby school building, pleading with God to bless all the work and worship of the day.

Then it was time for a cup of tea and a quick lunch, which had been prepared on Saturday, before the bell rang again — this time to call everyone to Sunday School. Not only the children, but all the adults also attended. John led the first part, giving a talk and asking questions about what they had learnt. Then they split up into classes. Margaret taught a large women's class and some of the native Christians also taught classes.

The classes lasted for about half an hour. Then, at about one o'clock they set off to take services in the villages. For this they split into two groups: one of the more mature native Christians and some of the teachers from Aneityum would go to one side of the island, while John and another group went to the other. They would hold a short service at each village, either in the open air or in the schoolroom when one had been built.

By sunset as John and the other preachers were making their way back homewards and feeling rather tired after their tour of the villages, they would hear drums being beaten in all the villages calling the people to evening prayers under the banyan-tree. The villagers would sing five or six hymns and in between there would be short times of prayer.

At the end of the day there would be an informal time of hymn-singing, Bible-reading and discussion at the mission house for all the young people and any of the villagers who wanted to join them. About nine o'clock John would suggest it was time for the villagers to go home, but usually they wanted to stay and join in the family worship, even though it was in English. 'Missi, we like the singing!' they would say. 'We understand a little. And we like to be where prayer is rising!'

At the end of the day the villagers assembled under the banyan tree for
evening prayers

The Lord's Day was a truly joyful day for the family and the other Christians on the island. It was not at all a dull or boring day, but a real time of praise and worship to God. Margaret always made sure that the family spent at least some part of the day together, free from visitors. After the services and classes were over, she would distribute picture books among the natives who wanted to stay, while the family sat on the shady verandah at the front of the house. There they would read books to the children, have a time of questions and answers, sing hymns together and enjoy the chance to talk to each other in English!

Weekdays too were busy. At first light drums were sounded in all the villages calling people to school. Once the first book in the Aniwan language had been printed, schools were set up in all the villages and people of all ages attended. The teachers from Aneityum took some classes, but in many of the villages the teachers were islanders whom John and Margaret had trained to teach the others. Classes had to be held at daybreak because as soon as the sun had dried off most of the heavy dew the natives would be off to work in their plantations.

A school house on Aniwa

When they had gone, John and the family would have breakfast. Then John would usually spend the rest of the morning working on his printing-press, or other jobs that needed to be done, or sometimes he would visit people who were ill. On two days a week Margaret had a class of women whom she taught sewing and to plait straw hats, which they were able to sell to the traders who called at the island. She also taught them reading and singing. The usual average for the class was about thirty women, but sometimes there were as many as fifty.

The natives would come home for lunch about two o'clock. After their hard work on the plantations they would take a dip in the sea. This was usually followed by a meal of coconuts or bread-fruits, or whatever else they had to hand. Then at three o'clock the bell would be rung again and the teachers and more advanced pupils would come for an hour and a half or so of teaching from John, while Margaret took a class for lessons in writing.

Then some of the islanders would go fishing while the women started preparing the evening meal, which was the main meal of the day. Around sunset the drums would be beaten and the day closed with village prayers held in the open air under the banyan trees.

Two nights each week, after the evening worship at the mission house, there would be an 'essay evening', when the native boys and girls who lived with John and Margaret would hand in essays they had prepared on some subject which interested them, or some incident which had happened on the island. John would read these out aloud, correcting any mistakes. They used to take great pride in preparing these essays and one day when the *Dayspring* had been sighted off the coast Margaret was surprised to find all fourteen of them crowded rounded the table after tea, busily writing by the light of the lamp. She asked why they did not wait till the next day, when they could write by daylight, but they begged her, 'O Missi, just let us sit here with the lamp till the worship, for there will be no time tomorrow when the vessel is here, and we must have our books written.'

On some of the other islands in the New Hebrides, however, life was very different for the missionaries and their lives were still in real danger. When the *Dayspring* arrived on its yearly visit early in 1872 it brought a group of Christian natives from Erromanga who had some very distressing news for John and Margaret and who begged to be allowed to stay on Aniwa because they were afraid to return home.

After the murder of George and Ellen Gordon on Erromanga some eleven years earlier, that island had been without a missionary for a while, but about the same time as John and Margaret came to live on Aniwa, George Gordon's brother James had come out from Canada to take up the work his brother had begun.

James Gordon

Over the years John and Margaret had come to know him well as a fellow-worker and to love him as a dear brother in the Lord. They were therefore deeply shocked and distressed to learn that James Gordon, like his brother before him, had now been murdered. Once again it was the old story of a missionary being blamed for bringing diseases to the islands, when really the fault lay not with the missionaries at all, but with the trading-ships that called at the island.

One day while James Gordon was hard at work translating the Acts of the Apostles into the Erromangan language a group of natives called at the house and asked him to come outside. When he did so, one of them struck him down with a tomahawk and killed him. John and Margaret learned afterwards that at the moment when he was interrupted he was translating the account of the stoning of Stephen, the first martyr, and had just reached the words: 'Lord, do not charge them with this sin.' Margaret wrote that the ink was still wet on the page when James was called outside to join the noble company of those martyred in the Lord's service.

Margaret also described the 'eerie feeling' it gave her to think of James being killed in that way by people just like those among whom they lived every day. For a while she was very nervous of being left alone with only natives for company. Her fears were not entirely groundless, for even though most of the islanders were friendly to the missionaries, there were still some who caused trouble from time to time.

On one occasion a man named Nourai attacked John, hitting him again and again with the barrel of his musket until the local women rushed in and stopped him. As the man ran off, John told the men, who had stood by watching without trying to intervene, 'If you do not now try to stop this bad conduct, I shall leave Aniwa and go to some island where my life will be protected.'

The next morning a party of about a hundred armed men arrived to escort John to Nourai's village, saying, 'We will find out why they sought your life, and we will rebuke their sacred man for pretending to cause hurricanes and diseases.' When they arrived at the village everyone gathered round while speeches were made on both sides. Taia, one of the men who had accompanied John, warned the local men, 'You think that Missi is here alone, and that you can do with him as you please! No! We are now all Missi's men. We will fight for him

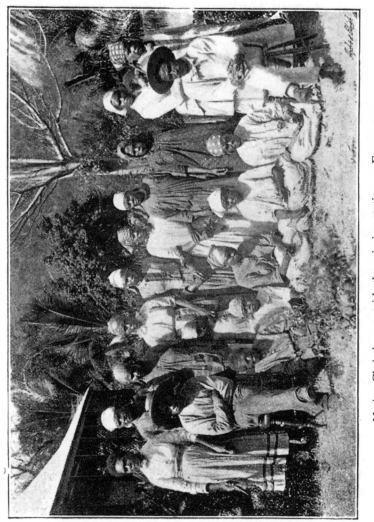

Native Christians outside the mission station on Erromanga

and his rather than see him injured. Everyone who attacks him attacks us. That is finished today!'

Then they made fun of the village sacred man, who claimed to be able to cause hurricanes and illnesses, but himself was suffering from a stiff knee. 'If he can make a hurricane, why can't he restore the joint of his own knee?' one of them asked. 'It is surely easier to do the one than the other!'

At that point the man's wife, who was a big, strong woman, turned on her husband and shouted at him for bringing this trouble on them all. Seizing a large coconut leaf, she began hitting him about the shoulders with it, saying, 'I'll knock the Tevil out of him! He'll not try hurricanes again!' Eventually John had to beg her to stop. The man then promised not to cause any more trouble. The whole scene ended peacefully, with the villagers making gifts of food and sugar-cane to John and his friends as a peace-offering.

Another time John was working on a plot of land he had bought near the mission house when a young chief named Youwili suddenly appeared and told him to stop. Then the chief strode to the fence around the mission house, broke it down and cut down some banana plants with his tomahawk. This was a traditional way of declaring war on someone.

Namakei and the other warriors gathered round, clutching their weapons. John warned them this had to stop, once and for all. 'Are you to permit one young fool to defy us all, and break up the Lord's work on Aniwa?' he asked. He told them they must find a fair and just way of punishing Youwili. Until they did, John said, he was not going to do anything more to help them, but would shut himself up in the house with his family till the mission ship called next time. Then, if they had still not done anything about Youwili, the family would sail away and leave them all! With that, he went into the house and shut the door.

The natives were very alarmed at the thought that John might go away. After a while Namakei and some other chiefs came to see him and asked how they should punish Youwili. 'Shall we kill him?' they asked.

'Certainly not,' John told them.

'What then? Shall we burn his houses and destroy his plantations? ... Shall we bind him and beat him? ... Shall we place him in a canoe, thrust him out to sea, and let him drown or escape as he may?'

To all these suggestions John answered, 'No.' By now the chiefs had run out of ideas, so he put forward a proposal of his own: 'Make him, with his own hand and alone, put up a new fence and restore all that he has destroyed; and make him promise publicly that he will cease all evil conduct towards us. That will satisfy me.'

When the chiefs reported back to the others, they all burst out laughing. Then everyone shouted out, 'It is good! It is good! Obey the word of the Missi!' So they went off to find Youwili and told him what they had decided. He was surprised to be let off so lightly, but agreed.

By daybreak next morning Youwili was hard at work on the fence and by the end of the day it was all repaired; in fact it was even better than before he damaged it. As he worked, some of the other natives teased him saying, 'You found it easier to cut down Missi's fence than to repair it again. You will not repeat that in a hurry!' Youwili did not answer and when the job was finished he left without saying a word.

Time passed, during which John and the family prayed every day that God would work in Youwili's heart and bring him to faith in the Lord Jesus. At last God answered their prayers and Youwili was saved. Instead of going around with a sullen expression on his face, now he was radiant with the joy of his new-found faith. His wife came to the mission house asking for a book and a dress, saying, 'Youwili sent me. His opposition to the worship is over now. I am to attend church and school. He is coming too. He wants to learn how to be strong, like you, for Jehovah and for Jesus!'

Youwili found learning to read difficult, but his wife helped him and together they came regularly to the class for those who wanted to join the church. Eventually John had the great joy of sitting down at the Lord's Table with both of them as brothers and sisters in Christ. He praised the Lord, who is able to change the hearts and lives even of those who are most opposed to the gospel.

It was after his first communion service that Youwili approached John with a problem. He waited for John under an orange tree growing near the mission house. 'Missi,' he said, 'I've given up everything for Jesus, except one. I want to know if it is bad, if it will make Jesus angry; for if so, I am willing to give it up. I want to live so as to please Jesus now... Missi, I have not yet given up my pipe and tobacco! Oh, Missi, I have used it so long, and I do like it so well; but if you say that it makes Jesus angry with me, I will smash my pipe now, and never smoke again!'

John was in a difficult position. He did not approve of smoking and the missionaries always encouraged the new converts to give it up. However, he knew that many Christians back at home or in Australia smoked and he did not believe it right to set a double standard.

He began by explaining his own views to Youwili: 'For my part, you know that I do not smoke; and from my point of view I would think it wrong in me to waste time and money and ... health in blowing tobacco smoke into the air... It could not possibly help me to serve or please Jesus better. I think I am happier and healthier without it. And I am certain that I can use the time and money, spent on this selfish and rather filthy habit, far more for God's glory in many other ways.'

'But,' he added, 'I must be true to you, Youwili, and admit that many of God's dear people differ from me in these opinions … and do not regard it as sinful. I will not therefore condemn these, our fellow-Christians, by calling smoking a sin … but I will say to you that I regard it as a foolish and wasteful indulgence, a bad habit, and that though you may serve and please Jesus with it, you might serve and please Jesus very much better without it.'

Youwili thought hard for a time and then replied, 'Missi, I give up everything else. If it won't make Jesus angry, I will keep the pipe. I have used it so long, and oh, I do like it!'

John remained firmly convinced that smoking was a bad habit for Christians, but he believed that, where the Bible did not clearly prohibit something as sinful, the new converts must be guided by their own consciences rather than just doing what the missionary told them.

To think about

You have read about the first Lord's Supper on the island of Aniwa. This meal of remembrance is important in our Christian life as it is one of the ways God has appointed for us to grow as Christians.

John was strict in determining who was permitted to sit at the Lord's Table. Who should be allowed to take part in the communion service? Who should be forbidden a seat at the Lord's Table?

The islanders generally loved and respected John and Margaret and it should be the same for us in our relationship with our pastor and his family. Your pastor and his wife have made many sacrifices in order to bring the gospel to you. They may have sacrificed a home of their own, as well as a well-paid and secure job, to serve Christ and his people. We should all appreciate what our pastors have done for us. Go out of your way to say, 'Thank you,' and give them encouragement when the occasion arises.

Youwili decided not to give up smoking his pipe, although John told him he thought he could serve the Lord better if he did not smoke. Many people today smoke cigarettes and damage their health. Some take illegal drugs which cause much harm. In all we do we must remember that our bodies are the temple of the Holy Spirit and as such should be cared for very carefully. God created us with glorious bodies. It is sinful to harm them and that means avoiding bad habits such as smoking, taking illegal drugs and heavy drinking.

There are some issues on which God has not given specific commands in the Bible and over which we have liberty of conscience. John felt that the question of smoking came into this category, so he left Youwili to make up his own mind. We too must respect others who hold views differing from ours, in those areas where there is no clear command in Scripture.

23.
The second 'Dayspring'

Although usually plenty of fruit and crops grew on the island, there were times when food was in short supply. On one such occasion, as John was passing a hut, he heard the father of the family giving thanks to God for the food he had provided. As John drew near he saw that they were sitting down to a meal of cooked fig-leaves.

At the mission, where they relied more on things such as flour and tea which had to be brought to the island from other countries, they were also feeling the shortage of food and hoping the *Dayspring* would soon arrive with fresh supplies. The orphan children came to John one day, saying, 'Missi, we are very hungry.' They asked if they could climb up into the fig-trees beside the mission house and eat some of the tender young leaves. When John said, 'Yes,' they scrambled up into the trees and were soon munching away happily like so many squirrels.

Every evening, during family prayers, they would pray for the ship to come, and each morning the boys would run down to the shore and look out for any sign of a sail. At last one morning, they came running back to the house to announce that a ship was coming. But they were not sure if it was the right one. 'Missi,' they told John, 'she is not our own vessel, but we think she carries our flag. She has three masts, and our *Dayspring* only two!'

The wreck of the *Dayspring* off Aneityum during a hurricane, 6
January 1873

It turned out that the *Dayspring* had been wrecked on a coral
reef during a storm and the mission had hired another ship, the
Paragon, to bring supplies to the islands.

As the first load of boxes from the *Paragon* were being
unloaded on the quayside, the children crowded round John.
'Missi,' they told him, 'here is a cask that rattles like biscuits!
Will you let us take it to the mission house?'

John agreed, so the boys promptly set off up the path,
rolling it along the ground in front of them as they ran. They
did not stop until they reached the door of the storehouse.
When John came back from the shore he found them all there,
waiting for him. 'Missi,' they said, 'have you forgotten what
you promised us?'

John pretended not to know what they wanted. 'What did
I promise you?' he asked.

They all looked at each other and whispered, 'Missi has
forgot!' Then they reminded him: 'You promised that when
the vessel came you would give each of us a biscuit.'

Rolling home the barrel of biscuits

John found a hammer and tools to knock the hoops off the cask and handed biscuits to each of the children. To his surprise, they all stood quietly waiting, holding their biscuits.

'What!' he asked. 'Why don't you eat? Are you expecting another?'

One of the oldest spoke up: 'We will first thank God for sending us food, and ask him to bless it to us all.'

By now John and Margaret had four children of their own: Bobby, Fred, Minn and Frank. At the end of March 1873 a baby girl, Lena (short for Helena), was born, but sadly she only lived a few days. The first few months of that year proved a difficult time for all the family. First there was a hurricane, which tore up trees and smashed windows in the house. A few weeks later an earthquake shook the island. Then both John and Margaret fell ill for some weeks. In fact they were both ill in bed when their baby died, and the teachers, helped by some of the native women, had to dig the grave and bury her. It was the two young boys, Bob and Fred, who had the responsibility of representing the family at the graveside, where their parents could hear their voices joining in the hymn-singing. At one point John was so weak he could not speak and everyone thought he was dying. For some time after he recovered he could only walk using crutches.

So the other missionaries decided that the family should spend some time in Australia and New Zealand, where they could receive medical treatment and relax in the cooler climate. It was also hoped that when John was well enough he could make arrangements to buy another ship to replace the *Dayspring*.

As soon as they landed in Sydney John consulted some friends there who agreed to buy the *Paragon* on behalf of the mission. This was a step of faith as they did not know where they were going to find the money, but they believed that it was God's work and he would supply the money needed.

Then a public meeting was called at which people were told of the need for money to meet the cost of buying the ship and making some necessary alterations to it. When the fund-raising was well under way John took his doctor's advice and sailed for New Zealand.

On board the same ship there were a party of men who were returning from the horse races in Melbourne. These men were constantly swearing and taking God's name in vain. John was very hurt to hear God's name used in that way and he prayed about what he should do. On the second day as they were all sitting at the table for a meal, he spoke up. 'Gentlemen, will you bear with me a moment?' he began. 'I am sure no man at this table wishes to wound the feelings of another or to give needless pain.'

Everyone turned and stared at him, but no one spoke as he went on: 'We are to be fellow passengers for a week or more. Now I am cut and wounded to my very heart to hear you cursing the name of my heavenly Father, and taking in vain the name of my blessed Saviour. It is God in whom we live and move, it is Jesus who died to save us, and I would rather ten times over you would wound and abuse me, which no gentleman here would think of doing, than profanely use those holy names so dear to me.'

An awkward silence followed John's words. Later the ship's captain sent for John and told him he too was a Christian and thanked him for the stand he had taken for the honour of God. After that day John never heard another oath all the time he was on the ship. When they arrived in New Zealand one of the men, who had at first been very angry with John for what he said, actually gave him an invitation to visit him at his home!

John felt much better by the time he landed in New Zealand, but he was not looking forward to the task of making fresh appeals for money for the ship. However, he was given a very warm welcome by the churches there and soon the money was flowing in. Once again the Sunday School children were encouraged to buy 'shares' in the ship, which had now been renamed *Dayspring II*, and by the time he returned to Sydney in March 1874 all the money had been raised to cover, not only the cost of the ship and the alterations to her, but also her running expenses for the next year!

Dayspring II

John and Margaret had now both fully recovered their health and when the *Dayspring II* next sailed for the islands they travelled on her, with their two younger children, glad to be going back to their home on Aniwa to take up the work there once more. Bob and Fred, however, were left behind in Australia, where several members of Margaret's family lived, and where they were to go to school.

Altogether John and Margaret lived on Aniwa for fifteen years, from 1866 to 1881. During all that time the island was their home and, apart from the occasional visits of passing trading-ships, their only real contact with the outside world was through the visits of the *Dayspring*, once or twice a year. They always eagerly looked forward to the ship's arrival, especially as it brought letters from friends and family, as well as fresh supplies of flour, biscuits, tea, fresh oranges and other things they needed.

Both John and Margaret found the separation from their children very hard to bear and when the cry 'Sail O' went up, to let everyone know the *Dayspring* had been sighted out at sea, their first thoughts were for news of Bob, Fred and, in time too, Minn, away at school in Australia.

Each year too the ship would sail around the islands taking missionaries to and from Aneityum for the annual mission conference. Margaret in particular enjoyed the chance to spend a few days in the company of the other missionary wives, chatting and catching up on each other's news and enjoying a brief few days of holiday together in the midst of their busy lives.

But when they sailed for Australia in August 1881 with Frank and his younger brothers, Jay (James) and baby John, they were not just leaving for a holiday, or a family reunion, but to start another stage in their ministry, in which much more of John's time would be taken up in travelling and preaching on behalf of the mission. From that time onwards they would mainly be based in Australia, although they made several visits back to the islands.

Margaret wrote of how hard it was to leave 'dear old Aniwa', and the house which had been the family home for so long and the garden they had planted. But even more heart-breaking was saying farewell to the islanders whom they had come to love.

Hutshi

The parting was all the harder because they left behind on Aniwa the graves of two of their children — the baby Lena and little Walter, a lively little boy who had died unexpectedly at the age of two, only a few months before they left the island. The night before they sailed, Hutshi, one of the native girls who had lived with them at the mission, told her, 'You your-selves may go away, Missi, and leave us; but you can't rob us of the little ones in the graves. These two are ours; they belong to the people of Aniwa; and they will rise with the Aniwans in the great Resurrection day, and they will go with us to meet with Jesus in his glory!'

To think about

John once again showed his courage in speaking out against the swearing and blasphemy he heard. Read the commandments as they are recorded in Exodus 20 and think about them. They speak of the majesty and holiness of our God and must be the law we obey at all times.

We are to stand firm for the things of God. The people respected John for his stand. Sad to say, in our age, most Christians keep their mouths closed rather than risk causing a disturbance when Christ is being humiliated.

No one enjoys being disliked. What should Christians do when they are confronted by situations such as the one in which John Paton found himself when Christ's name was being blasphemed?

24.
The Christians of Aniwa

In their years on Aniwa John and Margaret were greatly helped in their work for the Lord by native Christians. As time went on, and the converts grew in their knowledge of the Lord, they were able to accept more of the responsibility in the church, in the schools and in taking the gospel to others, until by the time John and Margaret left for Australia, the local Christians were able to take over most of the work in the church and the schools, with only occasional visits from John or other missionaries.

All the islanders who were truly converted to Christ were very keen, right from the start, to tell others about the Lord who had saved them. John was convinced that nothing that he said or did had as great an impact on the rest of the islanders as the living witness of these men and women. The people saw for themselves the great changes that had come about in their lives as a result of God's work in convicting them of their sin and causing them to turn away from their sinful ways and to believe in the Lord Jesus Christ as their Saviour.

One of John's earliest helpers on Aniwa was, of course, Chief Namakei and the story of his life is a real testimony to the grace of God in the salvation of sinners. Before his conversion Namakei had been a great warrior, for whom fighting and cannibalism were a normal part of everyday life.

The chief and teachers of Aniwa

But, from the very beginning of John's work on the island, Namakei began to show an interest in the teaching about the Lord Jesus Christ. The more he learned, the more he wanted to tell his people about the Lord. We have already seen how he preached to the people after the sinking of the well, publicly proclaiming that he intended to worship the one true God and encouraging them all to do the same. We also saw that he went on to be baptized and join the church as one of its first members.

When Namakei was very old and frail, he told John that the next time all the missionaries from the islands met together on

Aneityum for a conference he wanted to go along too to see them all and hear them talking about the work God was doing on the different islands. John was worried that the old man might die while he was away from home, and that if the ship returned without him the islanders would blame the missionaries for his death and turn against them once more.

However, Namakei was determined and so, the next time the *Dayspring* came to the island to take John and the family to Aneityum for a conference, Namakei went with them. He packed his few clothes and his precious booklets in a basket and boarded the ship. All his people stood on the shore to see him off, their tears flowing freely as he said goodbye and told them to 'Be strong for Jesus' and to always be loyal and kind to 'Missi', whether they ever saw him again or not.

The first few days on Aneityum went well. Everyone treated the old chief with great respect. He especially enjoyed going to the meetings and hearing about the Lord's work. His old heart was thrilled as he heard that one island after another was being won for the Lord Jesus and everywhere people were learning to worship him and sing his praises. He told John, 'Missi, I am lifting up my head like a tree. I am growing tall with joy!'

But after four or five days, Namakei knew he was dying. He asked someone to fetch John, who was in one of the meetings. When John came he said, 'Missi, I am near to die! I have asked you to come and say farewell. Tell my daughter, my brother and my people to go on pleasing Jesus, and I will meet them again in the fair world.'

John tried to encourage his dear Christian friend, saying God could still give him the strength to get well enough to go back home to his people, but Namakei knew he was about to die. He interrupted John in a faint whisper: 'O Missi, death is already touching me! I feel my feet going away from under me. Help me to lie down under the shade of that banyan tree.'

John gave Namakei his arm and supported his tottering footsteps as far as the tree, where the old man lay down thankfully in the cool shade and asked John to pray with him. 'I am going!' he whispered. 'O Missi, let me hear your words rising up in prayer, and then my soul will be strong to go.'

John attempted to pray, but he was so distressed at the thought of losing his dear friend — the very first of the islanders to be converted through his work — that he could hardly get the words out.

At last Namakei took hold of John's hand, pressed it to his heart and said, 'O my Missi, my dear Missi, I go before you, but I will meet you again in the home of Jesus. Farewell!' With those words on his lips Chief Namakei fell asleep in Jesus.

Namakei was buried there on Aneityum, and all the missionaries who had gathered for the conference stood around his grave, weeping at the loss of a true friend and brother in Christ. John would miss him greatly, but he also marvelled at the grace of God that had so transformed the life of a man who only a few years before had been a cannibal. He rejoiced that his old friend was now in glory and enjoying the Lord's own presence.

John was still concerned about his reception when the ship arrived back in Aniwa without Namakei on board. As the *Dayspring* approached the island, they could see all the people lining the shore, waiting for them. Among them were Namakei's daughter Litsi and his brother Kalangi. As soon as the ship came near enough for her to see who was on deck Litsi called out, 'Missi, where's my father? Is Namakei dead?'

When John answered, 'Yes. He died on Aneityum. He is now with Jesus in glory,' a great cry went up from the assembled people as they mourned the loss of their beloved chief. The ship slowly moved into the harbour and as soon as the passengers landed Litsi and Kalangi were waiting there to greet them. They shook hands with John and Margaret, welcomed them back and told them they had nothing to worry about. Through her tears, Litsi told them, 'We knew that he was dying, but we dared not tell you. When you agreed to let him go, he went round and took farewell of all his friends, and told them that he was going to sleep at last on Aneityum, and that at the Great Day he would rise to meet Jesus with the glorious company of the Aneityumese Christians. He urged us all to obey you and be true to Jesus. Truly, Missi, we will remember my dear father's parting word, and follow in his steps and help you in the work of the Lord!'

The other chief who had been interested in the work of the missionaries right from the early days was Naswai. He was chief of one of the inland villages and one of the most powerful men on the island. When he became a Christian he had no time for anyone who tried to cheat or be dishonest. He worked as hard as anyone at jobs that needed to be done around the mission and refused to accept any payment. His wife Katua was a very dignified lady, and the first woman on the island to begin wearing Western-style dress. She was a great help to her husband and a good example to the other women.

Naswai came to be a real helper to John in preaching and teaching the Word of God. For years one of his greatest delights was to carry the large pulpit Bible from the mission house to the church building each Lord's Day morning and to make sure that everything was ready for the service. He also became an elder in the church and the teacher in his local village school. He was himself an able preacher, and John particularly remembered him for his clever use of illustrations drawn from everyday life.

Once Naswai preached to a party of islanders from Fotuna who had come on the *Dayspring* to visit Aniwa and see for themselves the change that Christianity had brought to the island. He told them, 'Men of Fotuna, you come to see what the gospel has done for Aniwa. It is Jehovah the living God that has made all this change. As heathens, we quarrelled, killed and ate each other. We had no peace and no joy in heart or house, in villages or in lands; but we now live as brethren and have happiness in all these things.'

He went on to explain that the only person who can really tell others about the Christian gospel is one who 'loves Jesus … and walks with him and tries to please him'. He told the story of a chief on Erromanga who had once been to a feast on another part of the island where he tasted all kinds of delicious dishes, all of which he was told were made from coconuts. So when he went back home the chief took with him a large supply of coconuts for his own people to try. However, they did not know the right way to cook them, with the result that the coconuts were spoiled and everyone laughed at the chief saying, 'Our own food is better than that!' Naswai then explained the point of the story: 'Was the fault in the coconuts? No, but they were spoilt in the cooking! So your attempts to explain Christianity will only spoil it. Tell them that a man must live as a Christian, before he can show others what Christianity is.'

Naswai died in 1875, while John and Margaret were away visiting Australia and New Zealand. As he was dying he pleaded with his people to love and serve the Lord Jesus. He told them how Christ had completely changed his life and made him a 'new creature', saying he was perfectly happy to be going to be with his Saviour.

One of the next most powerful chiefs on the island after Namakei and Naswai was Nerwa. When John first came to his village Nerwa heckled him and tried to stop him preaching. 'It's all lies you come here to teach us, and you call it worship!' he shouted out one day as John was speaking. 'You talk of

Jehovah as if you had visited his heaven. Why, you cannot climb even to the top of one of our own coconut trees… You never saw that God; you never heard him speak; don't come here with any of your white lies, or I'll send my spear through you!'

But God used the witness of two young orphans from Nerwa's village to break down his opposition to the gospel. First, a little girl came to live at the mission, where she soon learnt to read and write. Whenever she went back to see her friends in the village she would tell them, in her simple way, what she had been learning about the Lord Jesus who had come to live on earth and die for sinners. Then a young boy came to be trained at the mission and he too used to go back and tell his people how kind John and Margaret were.

One day Nerwa's wife came to the service asking for some clothes and a book. 'Nerwa's opposition dies fast,' she told them. 'The story of the orphans did it! He has allowed me to attend the church, and to get the Christians' book.'

She went back to her village and told everyone about what she had seen and heard. Then some of the other women began to come too, and in time some of the men. Eventually Nerwa himself came to see what was going on. At first he sat at a distance, where he could just hear the singing. Then he gradually moved closer until he could also hear the preaching. Soon he was regularly attending the services, listening attentively and thinking seriously about all he heard. The Holy Spirit worked in his heart and he too became a new man in Christ. Once he had opposed the gospel and threatened to kill the missionaries, but now he was one of their greatest helpers, determined to win other local chiefs for Christ.

When Naswai died, Nerwa took over his duties of carrying the Bible to church and getting everything ready for the service. He became the teacher in his village school and in time was appointed an elder in the church, along with his friend Ruwawa, who was one of the people who had come to hear the gospel because of Nerwa's witness.

When Nerwa was approaching the end of his life he was so well loved by everyone that people from all parts of the island came to visit him during his last illness. As they sat around his bed, it was he who would read to them a passage from the Gospels in his own language. He would also pray for them and sing a verse of one of his favourite hymns, which spoke about going to be with Christ and the joys of heaven.

When he was on his deathbed Nerwa asked John to call the young people together. He told them, 'After I am gone, let there be no bad talk, no heathen ways. Sing Jehovah's songs, and pray to Jesus, and bury me as a Christian. Take good care of my Missi, and help him all you can. I am dying happy and am going to be with Jesus, and it was Missi that showed me the way...' Then he asked for a chapter of the Bible to be read and both he and John prayed. Finally, at his request, the Christians standing round his bed sang in their own language the words of the hymn, 'There is a Happy Land'. As they did so the old man pressed John's hand and slipped peacefully away to live in the land of which they were singing:

> There is a happy land,
> Far, far away,
> Where saints in glory stand,
> Bright, bright as day.
> Oh how they sweetly sing,
> 'Worthy is our Saviour King!'
> Loud let his praises ring,
> Praise, praise for aye...

After Nerwa's death, his place as teacher in the village school was taken by the husband of the orphan girl whose

witness years before had been used by God to overcome his
hostility to the gospel. The girl, now a young woman, was
herself a fine Christian and a great help to her husband.
Together they carried on the work of teaching the people in the
village to read and write as well as to love and serve the Lord
Jesus.

Namakei's daughter Litsi, who had grown up at the mission
with John and Margaret as one of their family, eventually went
with her husband to work as a teacher on Tanna, when at long
last another missionary was sent to that island, which John had
been forced to leave so many years before. She became one of

Litsi

a team who worked there faithfully for many years bringing
the gospel to that needy island.

Once, when John went to
visit her, she greeted him with
the words: 'O my father! God
has blessed me to see you
again. Is my mother, your dear
wife, well? And your children,
my brothers and sisters? My
love to them all!'

Then she went on to tell him:
'My days here are hard. I might be happy and independent as
Queen of my own Aniwa. But the heathen here are beginning
to listen. The Missi sees them coming nearer to Jesus. And oh,
what a reward when we shall hear them sing and pray to our
dear Saviour! The hope of that makes me strong for anything.'

It was the same hope that sustained John and Margaret
when things were difficult, keeping them strong in all their
long years of faithful service to the Lord.

John could tell the stories of many other men and women
of Aniwa whose lives God changed and who were brought to
repent of their sins and turn in faith to the Lord Jesus Christ,

the only Saviour of sinners. Every one of these stories bears witness to the glorious grace of the Lord Jesus Christ, who came into the world to live and die for sinners — even murderers and cannibals!

To think about

God forgave murderers and cannibals who repented and believed in Christ. What is repentance and why should God forgive anyone?

All humans are called to repentance and faith in Christ and this means a godly sorrow for sin and a turning from sin to a life of righteousness. Look at yourself and consider if you have really repented of your sins and made a break with any old sinful ways.

When we witness to Christ we need to tell people that God forgives all the sins of those who believe in him. This means that there is hope for the worst of sinners. Think of the apostle Paul before he was converted. He was involved in the killing of some Christians, but found forgiveness. He then loved and served the God who loved him and died for him.

Give some thought to what we owe to Christ because of his saving life and death.

25.
The 'King of the Cannibals'

By the early 1880s the Patons' work on the island of Aniwa had come to an end. The glorious gospel of the Lord Jesus Christ had broken down the hearts of cruel, murderous pagans and the name of Jesus was worshipped throughout the island. While continuing to maintain close links with the islanders, John was from that time onwards to spend much of his time travelling and speaking on behalf of the mission.

In 1884 he sailed once more for Britain. One of the main reasons for his journey was that once again money was needed for a new ship. By this time the age of sailing ships was drawing to its close and the missionaries had decided that a steamship was needed to replace the *Dayspring II*.

On his arrival in Scotland, John went to stay with his brother James, who was by now living in Glasgow, and, using James' home as a base, began a tour of churches which took him to many places in Ireland and England as well as to the churches in Scotland where he was already known.

As he spoke at meetings all over Britain, telling people about the work on the islands of the New Hebrides, money began to pour in. Many of the gifts were small amounts of money coming from the poorer people. At one meeting in Dundee he noticed a young Asian girl of about twelve years of age, who was sitting near the platform, listening to every word

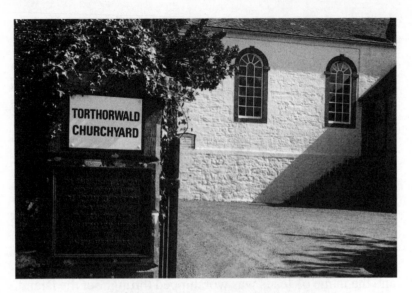

John Paton became a household name in Britain in his own lifetime. In his home village of Torthorwald he is commemorated on plaques on the churchyard gates.

he said. At the end of the meeting she stood up, bowed low in an Indian greeting and, taking four silver bangles from her wrist, told John, 'I want to take shares in your mission ship by these bangles, for I have no money, and may the Lord ever bless you!' At first John did not want to take them from her, but the lady who was with her urged John to do so, because if not, 'The dear girl will break her heart. She has offered them up to Jesus for your mission ship.'

The meeting that afternoon was a particular encouragement to John because that same morning he had had a very embarrassing experience. He had been asked to close the meeting with prayer and pronounce the benediction, but when he got as far as the words, 'May the love of God the Father...', his mind went blank and he could only think of the words in Aniwan! After an awkward silence he finished off with 'Amen', and sat down feeling hot and flushed and thinking no one would want to come and hear him again! He had become so used to thinking in the Aniwan language that the words now came to him more naturally in that language than in English! John spent much of the time between the two services in prayer to God for help and God answered his prayer, for that afternoon he had one of the largest and most interested congregations of his whole tour.

During that trip to Britain he also had the opportunity to meet some more famous people. He visited the orphan homes at Bristol founded by George Müller, met the leaders of the Bible Society, whose help was so important in the work of printing and publishing the Bible in the languages of the islanders, and even received an invitation from an earl and countess to address a private meeting at their castle.

The great London preacher, Charles Haddon Spurgeon, invited John to speak at a garden-party at his home, where the guests included Bible College students and other Christian workers. John had to smile when Mr Spurgeon, introducing the meeting, announced the speaker as 'the King of the Cannibals'! After the meeting Mrs Spurgeon presented John with a personal gift of a copy of her husband's writings on the Psalms, as well as a donation to the fund which she said came from 'the Lord's cows'. John afterwards learned that she kept a number of cows and that all the money she received from the sale of their milk, or of calves, was dedicated to the Lord's work.

John's trip to Britain lasted eighteen months. He had set out hoping to raise £6,000 for a new ship. By the time he returned he had raised £9,000, which meant that there was also enough money for the support of more missionaries. He was delighted that three new missionaries had also volunteered as a result of his trip. It was during this visit to his homeland that the University of Edinburgh awarded him the honorary degree of Doctor of Divinity.

On John's return to Aniwa, after an absence of four years, he woke very early on his first Lord's Day morning, before dawn, to hear the sound of hymn-singing. He jumped out of bed and called out, 'Have I slept in? Is it already church-time?' He found out that a number of the local Christians, including the chief and the teachers, had started a regular meeting at dawn each Lord's Day morning, for a time of prayer and praise before the services. He also discovered that they had continued to hold all the normal services and Bible Classes all the time he was away. He rejoiced when he heard that a large group of candidates, both young people and adults, was awaiting baptism and admission to the Lord's Table. He was delighted to see that the work was continuing without him and that the native Christians were taking on more responsibility in the life of the church.

By now John was in his sixties, an age when many people today would be thinking of retirement, but he was more active than ever, travelling all over the world to speak at meetings,

John and Margaret and their children, about 1887

telling everyone about the work of the mission and the wonderful things God had done on the islands of the New Hebrides.

One of the stories he used to tell was of one night, back in his early days on the islands,[1] when the mission house was surrounded by a crowd of hostile islanders who had come intending to kill John and his companions. The missionaries spent time in prayer to God and in the morning they found that all the natives had gone. Some years later John was talking to the leader of the men who had been hanging around outside that night and asked why they had not attacked and killed him and the other missionaries. The chief replied with another question: 'Who were all those men with you that night?' John was puzzled. As far as he knew there was no one outside the house that night, apart from the men who had come to attack. What exactly had happened that night would always remain a mystery, but John believed that God must have sent his angels to protect him and the other missionaries who were praying in that little house.

In 1892 John, Margaret and their daughter Minn set off on a tour that was to take them right round the world. Part of the purpose of this trip was to present an appeal to the government of the USA requesting an end to the dreadful trade in alcohol, drugs and weapons with the New Hebrides and other island groups in the Pacific Ocean.

They travelled via New Zealand, Samoa and Hawaii, before landing at San Francisco, where John was very distressed to see everyone going about their business as usual on the Lord's Day. As well as speaking at several meetings here, they had time to watch the seals basking on the rocks just outside the city and take a walk in a lovely garden with a fine view of the sea. Then it was on to Chicago, where a kind Christian who had been one of their fellow-passengers on the train took them on a tour of the city before they left for the Niagara Falls, *en route* for Canada.

Once more John spoke at meeting after meeting, both in Canada and the USA. By the time he presented his appeal to the president, many people had signed petitions supporting him and the daily newspapers were full of reports about John's tour and the work of the mission which he represented. During the time he was in the United States a new president was sworn in, so John actually made his appeal to two different presidents. He was also invited to a private lunch at the White House to talk about the work of the mission.

Eventually the matter of the prohibition of the trade in alcohol, drugs and weapons to the islands was left unsettled because France, Britain and America could not reach an agreeement concerning the course of action which needed to be taken. However, John continued holding meetings, both in the USA and Canada, telling everyone about the work of the mission.

Once, when on his way to hold a meeting, he had to get off the train at a lonely railway crossing, miles from any town, where he was expecting someone to meet him. It was a cold, rainy night and there was no one about. John walked about, trying to keep warm, and calling out every few minutes, but there was no answer. He began to shout 'Coo-ee' as loud as he could. At last he heard what sounded like an echo in the distance, gradually coming closer. It turned out that he had been put down at the wrong stop and the man who was to meet him was waiting at another crossing further down the line, until he heard John's call and came to investigate!

Another time the train broke down and the guard told all the passengers to get off and walk across the fields, but John decided to wait on the train. The men were worried that an express might come along the track at any moment and crash into the train. One man ran down the line ahead of the train, and another one back the way they had come, both frantically waving red flags and shouting. Meanwhile the engineers set to work, screwing, hammering and chiselling, until they managed to get half of the engine to work and the train crept slowly forward to the next station, with John still on board. Once more John was conscious that God had been watching over him and keeping him safe.

From North America, John travelled on to Britain, where he found he was now a household name, because since his last visit, ten years earlier, the first part of his *Autobiography* had been published. So many people wanted to come and hear the famous missionary for themselves that at one time he received 500 invitations at once and, unfortunately, some had to be disappointed. One invitation that had a special significance for John was signed by the ministers of all the Protestant churches in Dumfries, the town where he had attended church as a boy, just a few miles from the village where he had grown up and which held such happy memories for him.

John returned to Australia in 1894, after a trip which had lasted two years. Not long afterwards work began in the Scottish shipyards on the construction of the long-awaited steamship, *Dayspring III*. Sadly, this ship was to be wrecked after only completing three trips to the islands on behalf of the mission. She struck on a reef and the crew had to abandon ship. The captain and crew got into two boats. One boat made for a nearby island and those on board were soon rescued by a passing ship, but the other was at sea for two weeks, during which time it capsized more than once and the crew had to struggle on under a hot sun, with the food almost all gone. However, in God's goodness, the boat finally ran ashore on the coast of Queensland where all the crew were rescued. Though John was deeply upset at the loss of the *Dayspring*, he was full of praise to God that no lives were lost.

John G. Paton in 1894, at the age of seventy

John's overseas tours and the money coming in as result of the sale of his books also raised enough money to set up a fund for the support of more missionaries for the islands. It was his joy as an old man to see workers being settled on one island after another to preach the gospel of Christ to the natives. It must have thrilled him greatly to see two of his own sons among these new missionaries: Frederick on the island of Malekula and Frank and his wife on an island which would always have a very special place in John's affections—Tanna, where he himself had begun his work so many years before, and where his first wife and their child were buried.

Frank Paton

Although John himself never returned to Tanna to live there, as he had hoped, many of the young people whom he had trained on Aniwa later became mission workers on Tanna. They already knew the language and the links between the two islands were strong enough for them to be accepted more readily by the people of Tanna than missionaries from over-seas. So in a real way John's work on Aniwa was an important

The Scotch Church, Port Resolution, Tanna, dedicated 28 October 1891
as a memorial to the workers and work on that island.

step in taking the gospel to Tanna too. It was one of his greatest
joys in his last years on earth, before he passed into glory, to
see a Christian church formed on Tanna. Some of the very men
who had threatened his life and chased him from their island
now loved their old 'Missi' and rejoiced in the salvation they
had found in the Lord Jesus Christ.

The work of translating the Scriptures into the languages of
the different islands also went on. On one return visit to Aniwa
John was able to take with him the complete New Testament
translated into the language of the islanders.

For the last few years of his life John made his home in
Melbourne with his daughter-in-law. His beloved wife
Margaret died in 1905 and John himself passed away to be
with the Lord he loved and served on 28 January 1907, aged
eighty-three years.

As he looked back over his life in the closing pages of his
Autobiography he wrote, 'Oh that I had my life to begin again!
I would consecrate it anew to Jesus in seeking the conversion

TA FASAO EREFIA MA TAPU

O IESU KRISTO,

HEPE

NEISEREA IA JOANES.

NOPUKA AFASAO SORE, **1.**

I A ta nontafito neinofo ta Fasao, ma ta Fasao neinofo ia Atua, ma ta Fasao aia ko Atua.

2 Aia neinofo ia nontafito ia Atua.

3 Ane iotshi aia neimna, ma jimra tase foci neimna ane tase.

4 Ia aia aniamouri neinofo, ma aniamouri ra ko ta merama o tagata.

5 Ma ta merama kotshi ta noneate i apouri, ma ta pouri sekeiromana aia.

6 ¶ Tasi tatane Atua nikowna, tshana neigo Joanes.

7 Aia nimai tatane fakairo, keifakairo o ta Merama, pe tagatotshi neirogona aia ma fakarogrogo.

8 Aia kojimra ta merama ra, kaia nikowna keifakairo o ta merama ra.

9 Ta merama ra tamari, imna merama iotshi tagata koromai ia fanua wararonei.

10 Aia neinofo ia fanua wararonei, ma aia neimna fanua wararonei ma ta fanua waronei sekeiromana aia.

11 Aia nimai ia niana tagata, ma niana tagata sefakarogona aia.

12 Kaia ia faru o acre nifakarogrogo aia, iacre aia neitufwa tomatua keimna acre untariki o Atua, iacre, fakarogrogo ia tshana neigo;

13 Iacre sefarere o toto, mo o fenagaro o konouri, mo o fenagaro o tagata, kaia o Atua.

14 Ta Fasao neimna ia tatane, ma neinofo iacime ma acime neicitia tshana noniate, ta noniate hepe o aia ana Tamana niamo, aia nifonu o karofa erefisa ma o ta mari.

15 ¶ Joanes nifakairo o aia, ma nikova, nokoutucua, Tenei aia avou nifasao o aia, Aia komai wamuri avou, aia sore kage avou; ma aia neinofo mokagi avou.

16 Ma o tshana kofonu neitufwa acitiotshi, ma karofa o tshana karofa.

17 Ma ta fasao tapu neitufwa ia Moses, kaia karofa ma tamari niromai ia Iesu Kristo.

18 Jimra tasi tatane neicitia Atua ituai mo milow wararonei, ta Nontariki tasi ana, aia neinofo ia ta fatfata o Tamana, aia nifakairo tagata o aia.

19 ¶ Tenei fasao Joanes neitucua iateia, nopogera tagata Juteia nikowna fakow tapu ma fakow o Livai ia Jerusaiem keifakowia aia, Akoi akai?

20 Aia neitucua, ma sekoveteia; kaia neitucua, Avou jimra ta Kristo.

21 Acre nifakowia aia, Tiaha? Akoi Elija mo? Aia neitucua, avou jimra aia. Akoi ta profeta ra mo jimra? Aia neitucua, Jimra.

22 Iai acre neitucua iateia, Akoi akai? pe acime fakairo acre nikowna acime. Taha akoi koutucua akai akoi?

23 Aia neitucua, Avou ta norio o tasi nokotapa ia tugogou, Penpena totonu ta teretu o Ihova, hepe ta profeta Aiseia neitucua.

24 Ma acre nikowna iateia faru o tagata Afarasi.

25 Acre nifakowia aia, neitucua iateia, Tiaha akoi baptiso tagata, pe akoi jimra ta Kristo ra, mo Elaija, ma jimra tera profeta.

The first page of John's Gospel from the New Testament in the Aniwan language published in 1898.

Reproduced by courtesy of the British and Foreign Bible Society of the remaining cannibals on the New Hebrides. But since that may not be, may he help me to use every moment and every power still left to me to carry forward to the uttermost that beloved work.' Those words summarized his life and work.

He went on to say that the Lord had his own people, chosen and loved from eternity, among these primitive and cruel tribesmen and women, and he looked forward to seeing thousands of them joining in the worship and glory of heaven. 'Doubtless,' he wrote, 'these poor degraded savages are a part of the Redeemer's inheritance, given to him in the Father's eternal covenant, and thousands of them are destined through us to sing his praise in the glory and the joy of the heavenly world!'

He also praised the Lord for leading and guiding him throughout his life. He considered it to have been a wonderful privilege to have been used by God to bring the gospel to these islanders.

His closing words expressed the hope that the account of his life would be used to stir up a greater interest in the work of missions among God's people, and perhaps even to lead some of his readers to consecrate their own lives to missionary work: 'And should the record of my poor and broken life lead anyone to consecrate himself to mission work at home or abroad that he may win souls for Jesus, or should it even deepen the missionary spirit in those who already know and serve the Redeemer of us all — for this also, and for all through which he has led me by his loving and gracious guidance, I shall, unto the endless ages of eternity, bless and adore my beloved Master and Saviour and Lord, to whom be glory for ever and ever.'

---

1. This story is told in *Angels*, by Billy Graham. It is included here, rather than earlier in the book, because there is no record of it in the *Autobiography* and it is not clear at exactly what point in John's life this incident occurred

To think about

John spent much time and energy travelling the world getting help for missionary work. He met many important people, none of whom was better known in his day than C. H. Spurgeon. Spurgeon was a godly man, who had a keen sense of humour, as he showed when he called John Paton 'the King of the Cannibals'.

John's work was known worldwide, especially through the autobiography he wrote. Why should John Paton be remembered in our age?

From John's story we learn about the God he loved and served faithfully. What should this teach us who live at the conclusion of the twentieth century?

Index

Note: Figures in italic refer to illustrations